MW00935955

WISDOM FOR EACH DAY

Inherited from my Great-Grandfather

Book Two: Janine Turner's Front Porch Philosophy

© 2017 Janine Turner.

Janine Turner
Wisdom for Each Day: Inherited From My Great-Grandfather

All rights reserved. No part of this publication may be reproduced, stored in a retrieval system or transmitted in any form or by any means, electronic, mechanical, photocopying, recording or otherwise without the prior permision of the publisher or in accordance with U.S. Copyright Act of 1986.

Interior Design and Layout by: Juliette Turner

Edited by: Juliette Turner

Cover Design by: Michelle Burgess Wood

ISBN-10: 1981982809

ISBN-13: 978-1981982806

Distributed by: Amazon.com

Books by Janine Turner

Holding Her Head High
Twelve Single Mothers Who Championed Their Children & Changed
History

A Little Bit Vulnerable:
On Hollywood, God, Sobriety, & Politics

Artificial Intelligentsia vs. Primal Sense
Ten Steps to Reclaiming You

Podcasts by Janine Turner

God on the Go: Your Daily One-Minute Inspiration
Subscribe for your daily email/text: www.JanineTurner.com

Front Porch Philosophy
Visit YouTube.com to find Janine Turner's Front Porch Philosophy

Janine Turner's Social Media

Janine Turner Fan Page on Facebook

Janine Turner's Front Porch Philosophy on YouTube

Dedicated to Juliette,

My partner in purpose

WISDOM FOR
EACH DAY

SELECT QUOTATIONS

"Faith is the bird that feels the light and sings when the dawn is still dark."

RABINDRANATH TAGORE, INDIAN WRITER & POET

"Until a man has found God, he begins at no beginning and works to no end."

HERBERT GEORGE WELLS, ENGLISH AUTHOR

"Nothing splendid has ever been achieved except by those who dared believe that something inside them was superior to circumstances."

BRUCE BARTON, AMERICAN AUTHOR & POLITICIAN

"God brings men into the deep waters not to drown them, but to cleanse them."

JOHN HILL AUGHEY, AMERICAN ABOLITIONIST

"Disappointment is the nurse of wisdom."

SIR BOYLE ROCHE, IRISH POLITICIAN

"He who will not reason, is a bigot; he who cannot, is a fool; and he who dares not, is a slave."

WILLIAM DRUMMOND, 17TH CENTURY SCOTTISH POET

"Life can be only understood backwards, but it must be lived forwards."

SØREN KIERKEGAARD, DANISH PHILOSOPHER

"You can't hold a man down without staying down with him."

BOOKER T. WASHINGTON, AMERICAN EDUCATOR

"Life is the childhood of our immortality."

JOHANN WOLFGANG VON GOETHE, GERMAN WRITER

"Make it a rule of life never to regret and never to look back. Regret is an appalling waste of energy; you can't build on it; it's only good for wallowing in."

Katherine Mansfield, New Zealand writer

"There is so much good in the worst of us, and so much bad in the best of us, that it ill behooves any of us to find fault with the rest of us."

James Truslow Adams, American writer

"Never go out to meet trouble. If you will just sit still, nine times out of ten someone will intercept it before it reaches you."

Calvin Coolidge, 30th U.S. President

"I regret often that I have spoken, never that I have been silent."

Pubilius Syrus, Latin writer

My great-grandfather, Richard Hayes Burgess, and me.

INTRODUCTION

When my daughter, Juliette, graduated from high school and prepared for college, we embarked on the traditional great purge of the attic and storage unit. Amongst eighteen years of Juliette's baby furniture and toys, I found many of my old trunks; trunks stuffed with inherited familial prize possessions from generations of yore. Among the many wonders that I discovered in the dusty, old trunks was an old compilation of 365 typewriter typed and hand crafted epigrams. I was awed by their uniqueness and originality. As I perused this treasure trove assemblage of delightful and profound sayings, I instantly attributed the compilation to my beloved great-grandfather, Richard Hayes Burgess. Much of the wisdom in the collection was of his era (1885-1976) and the philosophers, leaders and poets of antiquity were those that his mind would relish.

I have always believed that my great-grandfather, with whom I had a special bond when he was alive, is my guardian angel. He always had a twinkle in his eye when he greeted me, taking me by the hand to pick pecans or to inspect his hydroponic garden. The last time I saw my ninety-year-old patriarch, I concluded the visit with the common salutation, "Good-bye, great grandfather," to which he replied, "You never say good-bye, you say 'see ya!'" I was thirteen years old, but I have never forgotten that moment or the poignancy of what he said to me.

I now know why he said it. He is still with me. He still sees me. I still feel him. Our bond is deepened by our likenesses which have become more rich and more clear through the years. He was a seeker of truth, an entrepreneur, an inventor and a writer. Amongst being a Major in the Army Airforce during World War II, he invented wings for man, cedar ashtrays, toothpaste rollers and many more things for which he wrote thorough reports and sent to the Smithsonian! He also wrote greeting cards and many short stories. His mind was always active and he was always creating. Though I have not invented wings for man, I too, am seldom still, always seeking and always creating. I loved him very much and I still do.

Wisdom for Each Day, Inherited from my Great Grandfather contains a collection of 365 sayings that you have likely never heard: historic, fresh, uplifting, soulful and funny - from sages across the globe and throughout the centuries. To keep the integrity, and to emphasize the genuineness, I have left all of the maxims in their original order. I was, however, drawn to discover more about the philosophers, writers and leaders accredited in this collection. Thus, I have included brief bios for each of the authors of the quotes. I believe that this added perspective deepens the wisdom and augments the impact.

Juliette, now a sophomore in college, is following suit as a seeker of truth and a professional writer. It is with a full heart and endless gratitude that I acknowledge and thank her for the loving devotion and patient diligence she exhibited in researching the bios for all of the little known but brilliant sages. I also thank her for her clever and artistic interior design. Her work ethic is unparalleled. She is my partner in purpose. Her great, great grandfather is proud of her! An added bonus is that the cover was designed by my talented cousin, Michelle Burgess Wood, who is Richard Hayes Burgess's great-great-granddaughter.

Enjoy your *Wisdom for Each Day, Inherited from my Great Grandfather*. I am inspired for the whole day every day and I believe you will be, too!

"Wings for Man" invented by my great-grandfather Burgess, tested by his son-in-law, Lloyd Welch.

January 1

The New Year is not present with us, only a new day ... Each day is a white page to be written; write it beautifully, and the book of the year will be beautiful.

J. H. Bliss

JOHN HOMER BLISS (1842-1922)
American historian and author.

Wisdom for
Each Day

JANUARY 2

Faith is the continuation
of reason.

William Adams

WILLIAM ADAMS (c. 1706 – 1789)
navigator, merchant, adventurer,
and the first Englishman to visit
Japan.

January 3

After the rain cometh the fair weather.

Aesop

Aesop (620 BC - 564 BC) fableist and story teller credited with a number of fables now collectively known as Aesop's Fables.

JANUARY 4

Our faith in God helps us meet whatever may come our way.

B. Albritton

The identity of B. Albritton and the history of this epigram is unknown.

JANUARY 5

Often the test of courage
is not to die but to live.

Vittorio Alfieri, <u>Orestes</u>

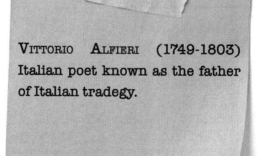

VITTORIO ALFIERI (1749-1803)
Italian poet known as the father
of Italian tradegy.

Wisdom for
Each Day

JANUARY 6

Obedience to his will today
means that God assumes
the responsibility for
our tomorrow.

C. L. Allen

CHARLES LIVINGSTONE ALLEN
(1913-2005)
Christian author and ordained
minister in the United Methodist
Church.

January 7

He who has health has hope, and he who has hope has everything.

Arabian Proverb

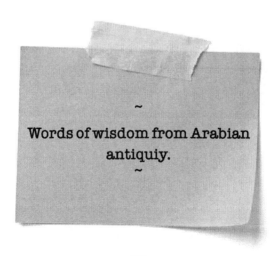

~

Words of wisdom from Arabian antiquiy.

~

Wisdom for
Each Day

JANUARY 8

A tree depicts divinest
plan, but God himself
lives in a man.

Joyce Kilmer

JOYCE   KILMER   (1886-1918)
American poet and writer well-
known for his religious writings.

January 9

You are a free person. I am so happy because in your freedom you choose me to be your friend.

Susan Polis Schutz

SUSAN POLIS SCHUTZ
(1944-present)
American poet and co-founder of Blue Mountain Arts, a greeting card and book publishng company.

Wisdom for
Each Day

JANUARY 10

The great essentials of happiness are something to do, something to love, and something to hope for.

Joseph Addison

JOSEPH ADDISON (1672-1719) English playwright, essayist, and politician.

JANUARY 11

The friends who are the most stimulating to us are those who disagree with us … It is they whose ideas we should ponder.

Cornelia James Cannon

CORNELIA JAMES CANNON
(1876-1969)
American feminist reformer and best selling author.

Wisdom for
Each Day

January 12

The world is not interested in the storms you encountered, but did you bring in the ship?

William McFee

WILLIAM McFEE (1881-1966)
English nautical writer.

JANUARY 13

Do not worry about what people are thinking about you ... for they are not thinking about you. They are wondering what you are thinking about them.

Anonymous

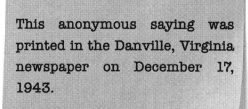

This anonymous saying was printed in the Danville, Virginia newspaper on December 17, 1943.

Wisdom for
Each Day

JANUARY 14

When wealth is lost,
          nothing is lost;
When health is lost,
          something is lost;
When character is lost,
          all is lost.

                    Billy Graham

BILLY GRAHAM (1918-present)
American Christian evangelist.

January 15

The flower that follows the sun does so even on cloudy days.

Robert Leighton

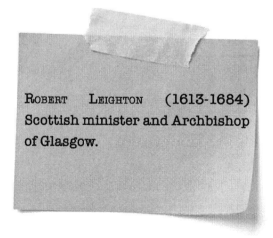

ROBERT LEIGHTON (1613-1684) Scottish minister and Archbishop of Glasgow.

Wisdom for
Each Day

JANUARY 16

The best way out of a
difficulty is through it.

Will Rogers

WILL ROGERS (1879-1935)
American entertainer and
comedian.

JANUARY 17

Prosperity makes friends
and adversity tries them.

Publilius Syrus

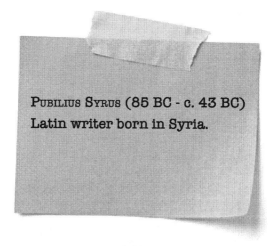

PUBILIUS SYRUS (85 BC - c. 43 BC)
Latin writer born in Syria.

Wisdom for
Each Day

JANUARY 18

Don't walk in front of me,
        I may not follow,
Don't walk behind me,
        I may not lead,
Walk beside me, and just be
        my friend.

Albert Camus

ALBERT CAMUS (1913-1960)
French journalist, philosopher,
and author.

JANUARY 19

If you can't get everything
you want, think of the
things you don't get that
you don't want.

Anonymous

This anonymous saying has been
attributed to ART BUCHWALD (1925-
2007), American humorist and
columnist for the Washington
Post.

Wisdom for
Each Day

JANUARY 20

What I do today is very
important because I am
exchanging a day of my
life for it.

Heartsill Wilson

HEARTSILL WILSON (dates unknown)
Texan accountant and
motivational speaker from the
mid-1900s.

JANUARY 21

If all the year were playing holidays, to sport would be as tedious as to work.

William Shakespeare

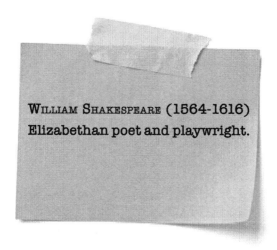

WILLIAM SHAKESPEARE (1564-1616)
Elizabethan poet and playwright.

JANUARY 22

Adversity introduces a man to himself.

Anonymous

This anonymous saying has been attributed to both scientist ALBERT EINSTEIN (1879-1955) and American journalist H.L. MENCKEN (1880-1956).

JANUARY 23

How much trouble he avoids who does not look to see what his neighbor says or does or thinks, but only to what he does himself, that it may be just and pure.

Marcus Aurelius

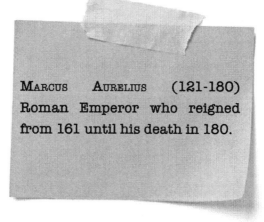

MARCUS AURELIUS (121-180) Roman Emperor who reigned from 161 until his death in 180.

January 24

God brings men into the
deep waters not to drown
them, but to cleanse them.

John Hill Aughey

John Hill Aughey (1828-1911)
American abolitionist and
Presbyterian preacher.

JANUARY 25

I am only one, but I am one.
I cannot do everything,
but I can do something.
What I can do, I ought to
do. And what I ought to
do, by God's grace I will
do.

Fredric William Farrar

FREDRIC WILLIAM FARRAR
(1831-1903)
Writer and cleric of the Church of
England.

Wisdom for
Each Day

January 26

Let us use our past mistakes and failures as building material for future success.

Anonymous

This anonymous saying was printed in The Willimington Messenger newspaper in North Carolina on April 20, 1898.

JANUARY 27

It isn't the thing you do,
It's the thing you leave undone
which gives you a bit of heartache
At the setting of the sun.

    Margaret Elizabeth Sangster

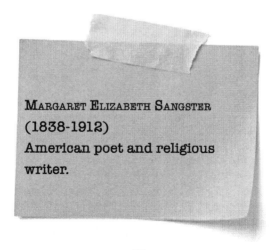

MARGARET ELIZABETH SANGSTER
(1838-1912)
American poet and religious
writer.

Wisdom for
Each Day

JANUARY 28

Help me, O Lord, to learn
the blessedness of silence.

Anonymous

This anonymous saying was
printed in the 1963 calendar of
The Christophers, founded by
Father James Keller of New York.

JANUARY 29

The willow which bends
to the tempest often
escapes better than the
oak which resists it.

Sir Walter Scott

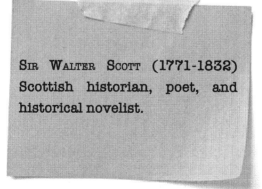

SIR WALTER SCOTT (1771-1832)
Scottish historian, poet, and
historical novelist.

Wisdom for
Each Day

JANUARY 30

Fear knocked at my door.
Faith opened that door.
And no one was there.

Anonymous

This anonymous saying was
printed in an Ann Landers
column found in the San Antonio
Express on June 14, 1967.

JANUARY 31

A cheerful heart and a
    smiling face
Put sunshine in the
    darkest place.

                    Anonymous

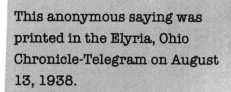

This anonymous saying was
printed in the Elyria, Ohio
Chronicle-Telegram on August
13, 1938.

FEBRRUARY 1

Parents who wish to train up their children in the way they should go must go in the way in which they would have their children go.

Sir Francis Bacon

SIR FRANCIS BACON (1561-1626) English philosopher, statesman, scientist, and orator. He served both as Attorney General and as Lord Chancellor of England.

Wisdom for
Each Day

FEBRUARY 2

If we begin with the certainties, we shall end in doubts, but if we begin with doubts, and are patient in them, we shall end in certainties.

Sir Fancis Bacon

SIR FRANCIS BACON (1561-1626) English philosopher, statesman, scientist, and orator. He served both as Attorney General and as Lord Chancellor of England.

FEBRRUARY 3

Learn to pause — or nothing worthwhile can catch up with you.

Dorothy Ballard

DOROTHY BALLARD
(dates unknown)
American author and journalist from the mid-1900s.

FEBRUARY 4

Hope is a light diet, but
very stimulating.

Honoré de Balzac

HONORÉ DE BALZAC (1799-1850)
French novelist and playwright.

FEBRRUARY 5

I live for those who love me, for
those who know me true;
For the heaven that smiles above
me, and waits my spirit too;
For the cause that lacks assistance,
For the wrong that needs resistance.
For the future in the distance and
the good that I can do.

George Linnaeus Banks, <u>My Aim</u>

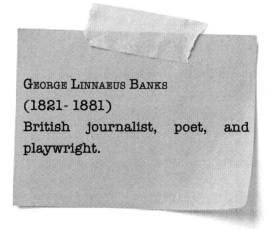

GEORGE LINNAEUS BANKS
(1821- 1881)
British journalist, poet, and
playwright.

Wisdom for
Each Day

FEBRUARY 6

The reason why birds can fly and why we can't is simply that they have perfect faith, for to have faith is to have wings.

James Matthew Barrie,
The Little White Bird

JAMES MATTHEW BARRIE
(1860-1937)
Scottish novelist and playwright
who created Peter Pan.

FEBRRUARY 7

Not in doing what you like, but in liking what you do that is the secret of happiness.

James Matthew Barrie

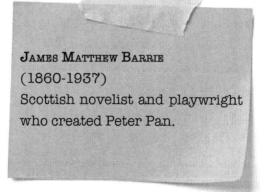

JAMES MATTHEW BARRIE
(1860-1937)
Scottish novelist and playwright who created Peter Pan.

Wisdom for
Each Day

FEBRUARY 8

Life is a long lesson in
humility.

James Matthew Barrie,
Little Minister

JAMES MATTHEW BARRIE
(1860-1937)
Scottish novelist and playwright.
who created Peter Pan.

FEBRRUARY 9

Wrinkles should only indicate where smiles have been.

Ethel Barrymore

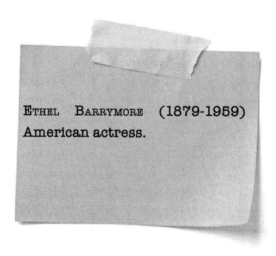

ETHEL BARRYMORE (1879-1959) American actress.

February 10

Making up your mind is like making a bed; it usually helps to have someone on the other side.

Gerald Horton Bath

GERALD HORTON BATH
(dates unknown)
American author from the mid-1900s.

FEBRRUARY 11

Victories that are cheap are cheap. Those only are worth having which come as the result of hard fighting.

Henry Ward Beecher

HENRY WARD BEECHER
(1813-1887)
American Congressional
clergyman and brother of
Harriet Beecher Stowe.

FEBRUARY 12

Do not look back on happiness or dream of it in the future. You are only sure of today; do not let yourself be cheated out of it.

Henry Ward Beecher

HENRY WARD BEECHER
(1813-1887)
American Congressional
clergyman and brother of
Harriet Beecher Stowe.

FEBRRUARY 13

God pardons like a mother,
who kisses the offense into
everlasting forgetfulness.

Henry Ward Beecher

HENRY WARD BEECHER
(1813-1887)
American Congressional
clergyman and brother of
Harriet Beecher Stowe.

FEBRUARY 14

It's love, it's love that
makes the world go round.

French song

French translation: L'amour,
l'amour fait tourner le monde.

FEBRRUARY 15

Fall down seven times—get
up eight.

Japanese Proverb

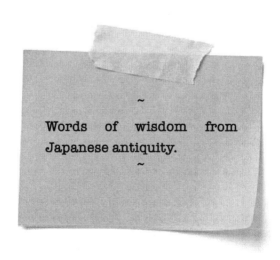

~

Words of wisdom from
Japanese antiquity.

~

Wisdom for
Each Day

FEBRUARY 16

The best cure for worry,
depression, melancholy,
brooding is to go
deliberately forth and try
to lift with one's sympathy
the gloom of somebody else.

Arnold Bennett

ARNOLD BENNETT (1867-1931)
English novelist, playwright, and
essayist.

FEBRRUARY 17

A man without mirth is like a wagon without springs, in which one is caused disagreeably to jolt by every pebble over which it runs.

Henry Ward Beecher

HENRY WARD BEECHER
(1813-1887)
American Congressional clergyman and brother of Harriet Beecher Stowe.

FEBRUARY 18

The reason why the Ten Commandments are short and clear is that they were handed down direct, not through several committees.

Dan Bennett

This quote from Dan Bennett was printed in the Van Nuys, California newspaper on October 11, 1951.

FEBRRUARY 19

How desperately difficult
it is to be honest with
oneself. It is much easier
to be honest with other
people.

Edward Fredric Benson

EDWARD FREDERIC BENSON
(1867-1940)
English novelist, biographer, and
archaeologist.

Wisdom for
Each Day

FEBRUARY 20

Blessed are those who can give without remembering and take without forgetting.

Elizabeth Charlotte Lucy, Princess Bibesco

ELIZABETH CHARLOTTE LUCY (1897-1945) Daughter of a British Prime Minister and the wife of Romanian Prince Antoine.

FEBRRUARY 21

Life's greatest achievement is the continual remaking of yourself so that at last you know how to live.

Dr. Smiley Blanton & Norman Vincent Peale

SMILEY BLANTON (1882-1966) American psychiatrist and psychoanalyst.
NORMAN VINCENT PEALE (1898-1993)
American clergyman.

Wisdom for
Each Day

FEBRUARY 22

The greater our difficulties,
the more we need the help God
offers through his Spirit.

L.A. Bledsoe, Jr.

The identity of L.A. Bledsoe,
Jr. and the history of this
epigram is unknown.

FEBRRUARY 23

Doubt whom you will, but
never yourself.

Christian Nestell Bovee

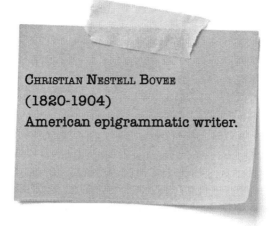

CHRISTIAN NESTELL BOVEE
(1820-1904)
American epigrammatic writer.

FEBRUARY 24

Gandhi had a sign reading:
'When you are in the right
you can afford to keep your
temper; when you are in the
wrong you can't afford to
lose it.'

Chester Bowles

CHESTER BOWLES (1901-1986)
American advertising executive
and Governor of Connecticut.

FEBRRUARY 25

The inevitable is only that
which we do not resist.

Justice Louis D. Brandeis

JUSTICE LOUIS D. BRANDEIS
(1856-1941)
United States Supreme Court
Justice from 1916 to 1939.

FEBRUARY 26

Do not pray for easy lives.
Pray to be stronger men. Do not
pray for tasks equal to your
powers. Pray for powers equal
to your tasks. Then the doing of
your work shall be no miracle.
But you shall be a miracle.
Every day you shall wonder at
yourself, at the richness of
life which has come to you by
the grace of God.

Reverend Phillips Brooks

REVEREND PHILLIPS BROOKS
(1835-1893)
American clergyman.

FEBRRUARY 27

I will seek each day to
find the manifestation of
God in those who pass my
way.

D.L. Brown

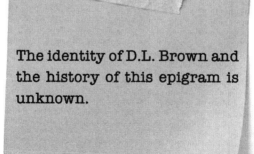

The identity of D.L. Brown and
the history of this epigram is
unknown.

FEBRUARY 28

You can do very little
with faith, but you can do
nothing without it.

Samuel Butler

SAMUEL BUTLER (1835-1902)
British author.

MARCH 1

The busy have no time for tears.

Lord Byron, <u>The Two Foscari</u>

LORD BYRON (1788-1824)
British Romantic poet and
author.

MARCH 2

I took a day to search for God,
And found Him not. But as I trod
By rocky ledge, through woods untamed,
Just where one scarlet lily flamed
I saw his footprint in the sod.

Bliss Carman, Vestigia

BLISS CARMAN (1861-1929)
Canadian poet.

MARCH 3

Our main business is not
to see what lies dimly at
a distance, but to do what
lies clearly at hand.

Thomas Carlyle

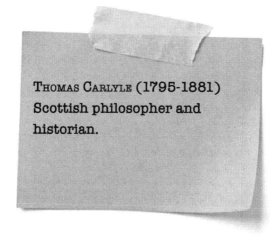

THOMAS CARLYLE (1795-1881)
Scottish philosopher and
historian.

Wisdom for
Each Day

MARCH 4

Little deeds of kindness
Little words of love
Make our earth an Eden
Like the heaven above.

> Julia F. Carney,
> <u>Little Things</u>

JULIA ABIGAIL FLETCHER CARNEY
(1823-1908)
American poet.

MARCH 5

The greatest gift of sight
is to see as Christ sees.

E. Clayton Calhoun, Jr.

E. CLAYTON CALHOUN, JR.
(1912-2009)
American Methodist minister,
educator, and missionary.

MARCH 6

Blessed are the missionaries
of cheerfulness.

Lydia Maria Child

LYDIA MARIA CHILD
(1802-1880)
American abolitionist, women's
rights activist, and author.

MARCH 7

O God, animate us to cheerfulness! May we have a joyful sense of our blessings, learn to look on the bright circumstances of our lot, and maintain a perpetual contentedness.

William Ellery Channing

WILLIAM ELLERY CHANNING
(1780-1842)
Unitarian minister and transcendentalist.

Wisdom for
Each Day

MARCH 8

Know the true value of time; snatch, seize, and enjoy every moment of it. No idleness, no laziness, no procrastination; never put off till tomorrow what you can do today.

Philip Dormer Stanhope,
Earl of Chesterfield
Letters to His Son

PHILIP DORMER STANHOPE
(1694 -1773)
4th Earl of Chesterfield and
British statesman.

MARCH 9

You must look into people as well as at them.

Philip Dormer Stanhope,
Earl of Chesterfield

PHILIP DORMER STANHOPE
(1694-1773)
4th Earl of Chesterfield and
British statesman.

MARCH 10

True contentment is a real, even an active virtue — not only affirmative but creative. It is the power of getting out of any situation all there is in it.

G.K. Chesterton

GILBERT KIETH CHESTERTON
(1874 -1936)
British writer, poet, and lay theologian.

MARCH 11

Loving means to love that which is unlovable, or it is no virtue at all; forgiving means to pardon the unpardonable, or it is no virtue at all. And to hope means hoping when things are hopeless, or it is no virtue at all.

G. K. Chesterton

GILBERT KIETH CHESTERTON
(1874-1936)
British writer, poet, and lay theologian.

Wisdom for
Each Day

MARCH 12

Nothing is so full of victory as patience.

Chinese Proverb

~

Words of wisdom from Chinese antiquity.

~

MARCH 13

Nothing splendid has ever been achieved except by those who dared believe that something inside them was superior to circumstances.

Bruce Barton

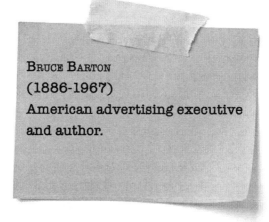

BRUCE BARTON
(1886-1967)
American advertising executive
and author.

Wisdom for
Each Day

MARCH 14

It is no use saying, "We are doing our best." You have got to succeed in doing what is necessary.

Winston Churchill

WINSTON CHURCHILL (1874-1965) Prime Minister of Great Britain from 1940 to 1945 and from 1951 to 1955.

MARCH 15

The greatest good you can
do for others is to reveal
their riches to themselves.

Benjamin Disraeli

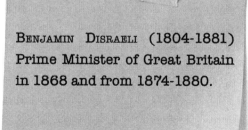

BENJAMIN DISRAELI (1804-1881)
Prime Minister of Great Britain
in 1868 and from 1874-1880.

MARCH 16

Man will wrangle for religion, write for it, fight for it, die for it; anything but live for it.

Charles Caleb Colton

CHARLES CALEB COLTON
(1780-1832)
British cleric and writer.

MARCH 17

The happiness of life is made up of a minute fraction — the little, soon forgotten charities of a kiss, or smile, a kind look, a heartfelt compliment — countless, infinitesimals of pleasurable and genial feeling.

Samuel T. Coleridge

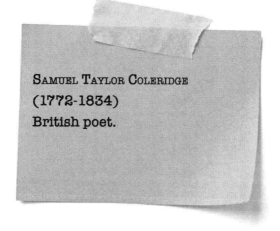

SAMUEL TAYLOR COLERIDGE
(1772-1834)
British poet.

Wisdom for
Each Day

MARCH 18

If you would take your possessions into the life to come, convert them into good deeds.

Charles Caleb Colton

CHARLES CALEB COLTON
(1780-1832)
British cleric and writer.

MARCH 19

There is no calm like that when
    the storm is done,
There is no pleasure keen as
    pain's release;
There is no joy that lies so
    deep as peace,
No peace so deep as that by
    struggle won.

                Helen Gray Cone

HELEN GRAY CONE (1859-1934) American poet and professor of English Literature at Hunter College in New York City.

Wisdom for
Each Day

MARCH 20

To know what is right and
not to do it is the worst
cowardice.

Confucius

CONFUCIUS (551 BC - 479 BC)
Chinese philosopher and
founder of Confucianism.

MARCH 21

Never go out to meet trouble. If you will just sit still, nine times out of ten someone will intercept it before it reaches you.

Calvin Coolidge

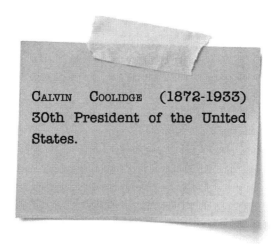

CALVIN COOLIDGE (1872-1933) 30th President of the United States.

MARCH 22

For we walk by faith, not by sight.

2 Corinthians 5:7

KING JAMES VERSION, HOLY BIBLE
The King James Bible was issued in 1611 by King James I and became the official Christian Bible for the Church of England.

MARCH 23

Be virtuous and you'll be happy? Nonsense! Be happy and you'll begin to be virtuous.

James G. Cozzens

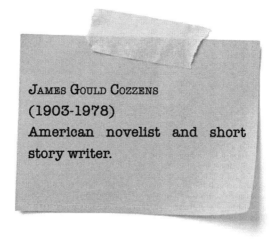

JAMES GOULD COZZENS
(1903-1978)
American novelist and short story writer.

Wisdom for
Each Day

MARCH 24

Gratitude is something of which none of us can give too much. For on the smiles, the thanks we give, our little gestures of appreciation, our neighbors build up their philosophy.

Archibald Joseph Cronin

ARCHIBALD JOSEPH CRONIN
(1896-1981)
Scottish novelist and physician.

MARCH 25

No one could tell me where my
    soul might be.
I sought for God, but God
    eluded me.
I sought my brother out, and
    found all three.

Ernest Crosby

ERNEST HOWARD CROSBY
(1856-1907)
American reformer and author.

Wisdom for
Each Day

MARCH 26

There are two kinds of men
who never amount to much—
those who cannot do what
they are told and those
who can do nothing else.

Cyrus H. K. Curtis

CYRUS H.K. CURTIS (1850-1933)
American magazine and
newspaper publisher.

MARCH 27

We're not primarily put on
this earth to see through
one another, but to see one
another through.

Peter De Vries

PETER DE VRIES (1910-1993)
American editor and satirical
novelist.

Wisdom for
Each Day

MARCH 28

The true way to soften one's trouble is to solace those of others.

Françoise d'Aubigné,
Marquise de Maintenon

FRANÇOISE D'AUBIGNÉ, MARQUISE DE
MAINTENON
(1635-1719)
Second wife of King Louis the
XIV of France.

MARCH 29

An optimist may see a light where there is none, but why must the pessimist always run to blow it out?

Michel de Saint-Pierre

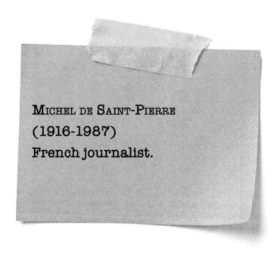

MICHEL DE SAINT-PIERRE
(1916-1987)
French journalist.

MARCH 30

When we have not what we
like, we must like what we
have.

Roger de Rabutin,
Comte de Bussy

ROGER DE RABUTIN, COMTE DE BUSSY
(1618-1693)
French memoirist.

MARCH 31

Being thoughtful of others all day is our everyday challenge.

Anonymous

This anonymous saying was printed in the Fayette County Leader in Iowa on September 4, 1969 and attributed to Dayavu Dhanapal of India.

APRIL 1

How foolish to doubt God's
existence simply because
we cannot see him.

M. Dorf

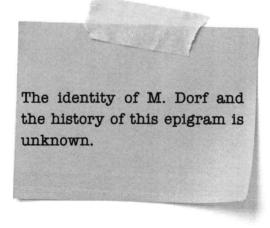

The identity of M. Dorf and
the history of this epigram is
unknown.

APRIL 2

If I can stop one heart from breaking,
I shall not live in vain;
If I can ease one life the aching,
Or cool one pain,
Or help one fainting robin
Unto his nest again,
I shall not live in vain.

Emily Dickinson

EMILY   DICKINSON   (1830-1886)
American poet.

APRIL 3

The most obvious lesson of
the gospel is that there is
not happiness in having
and getting, but only in
giving.

Henry Drummond

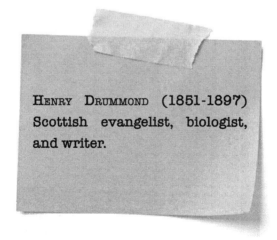

HENRY DRUMMOND (1851-1897)
Scottish evangelist, biologist,
and writer.

Wisdom for
Each Day

APRIL 4

He who will not reason, is
a bigot; he who cannot, is a
fool; and he who dares not,
is a slave.

William Drummond

WILLIAM DRUMMOND OF HAWTHORNDEN
(1585-1649)
Scottish poet.

APRIL 5

Few words in any language, are so charged with self-pity as loneliness. Yet, our first duty to society is to be somebody — that is to say, to be ourselves — and we can only be ourselves if we are often by ourselves.

Ernest Dimnet

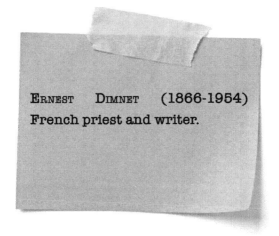

ERNEST DIMNET (1866-1954) French priest and writer.

APRIL 6

The little things are most worthwhile
A soothing word, a nod a smile
A listening ear, an open mind,
A gentle word so warm and kind.
The open heart that's quick to share
Another's thoughts, another's care
Though at times they seem so small
These little things mean most of all.

M. Goldsmith

The identity of M. Goldsmith
is unknown, but a similar
poem was written by Margaret
Lindsey.

APRIL 7

Thales was asking what was most difficult to man; he answered, "To know one's self."

Diogenes

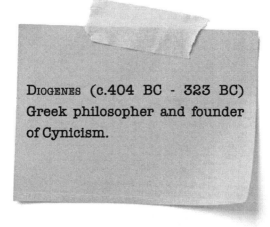

DIOGENES (c.404 BC - 323 BC) Greek philosopher and founder of Cynicism.

Wisdom for
Each Day

APRIL 8

To cultivate a garden is to
walk with God.

Christian Nestell Bovee

CHRISTIAN NESTELL BOVEE
(1820-1904)
American author.

APRIL 9

Inch, by inch, life's a cinch.

Anonymous

This anonymous saying was reportedly on the wall of Anne Bancroft's dressing room during the filming of Miracle Worker.

Wisdom for
Each Day

APRIL 10

Be not slow to visit the sick.

Book of Sirach 7:35

BOOK OF SIRACH (ECCLESIASTICUS)
Apocryphal book included in the
King James Bible until 1885 and
is still included in the Catholic
Bible.

APRIL 11

When down in the mouth,
remember Jonah. He came
out all right.

                    Thomas A. Edison

THOMAS ALVA EDISON (1847-1931)
American inventor.

Wisdom for
Each Day

APRIL 12

Time is really the only
capital that any human
being has, and the one
thing that he can't afford
to lose.

Thomas A. Edison

THOMAS ALVA EDISON (1847-1931)
American inventor.

APRIL 13

Prayer not only changes
things, it changes us.

                    M. Edwards

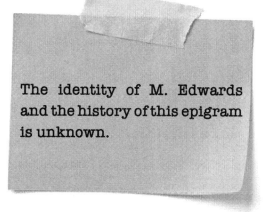

The identity of M. Edwards
and the history of this epigram
is unknown.

APRIL 14

The most we can get out
of life is its discipline
for ourselves, and its
usefulness for others.

Tyron Edwards

TYRON   EDWARDS   (1809-1894)
American theologian.

APRIL 15

Where there's a will, there's
a way.

English Proverb

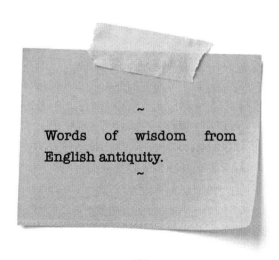

~

Words of wisdom from
English antiquity.

~

APRIL 16

Happiness is a perfume you cannot pour on others without getting a few drops on yourself.

Ralph Waldo Emerson

RALPH WALDO EMERSON (1803-1882) American essayist, poet, and lecturer.

APRIL 17

God offers to every mind
its choice between truth
and repose.

Ralph Waldo Emerson

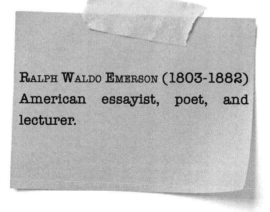

RALPH WALDO EMERSON (1803-1882)
American essayist, poet, and
lecturer.

APRIL 18

Adopt the pace of nature;
her secret is patience.

Ralph Waldo Emerson

RALPH WALDO EMERSON (1803-1882)
American essayist, poet, and
lecturer.

APRIL 19

All I have seen teaches me
to trust the Creator for
all I have not seen.

Ralph Waldo Emerson

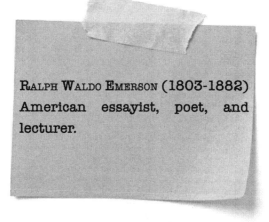

RALPH WALDO EMERSON (1803-1882)
American essayist, poet, and
lecturer.

Wisdom for
Each Day

APRIL 20

It is one of the most
beautiful compensations
of life that no man can
sincerely try to help
another without helping
himself.

Ralph Waldo Emerson

RALPH WALDO EMERSON (1803-1882)
American essayist, poet, and
lecturer.

April 21

The only way to have a friend is to be one.

Ralph Waldo Emerson

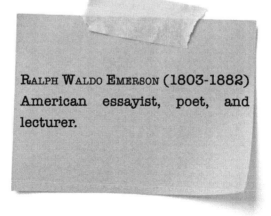

RALPH WALDO EMERSON (1803-1882) American essayist, poet, and lecturer.

Wisdom for
Each Day

APRIL 22

I am always content with
that which happens, for
I think that what God
chooses is better than what
I choose.

Epictetus

EPICTETUS (55 - c.135)
Greek Stoic philosopher.

APRIL 23

Contentment consists not
in great wealth but in few
wants.

Epictetus

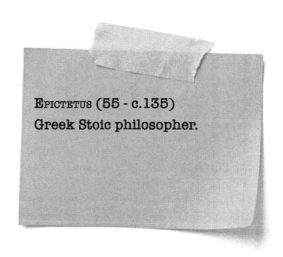

EPICTETUS (55 - c.135)
Greek Stoic philosopher.

APRIL 24

What do we live for if not
to make life less difficult
for each other?

George Eliot

GEORGE ELIOT (1819-1880)
The pen name for Mary Anne
Evans: British novelist, essayist,
and translator.

APRIL 25

Keep a smile on your face till 10 o'clock and it will stay there all day.

Douglas Fairbanks

DOUGLAS FAIRBANKS (1883-1939) American actor, director, and producer.

Wisdom for
Each Day

APRIL 26

To go on cheerfully with a petty round of little duties, to smile for the joy of others when the heart is aching. Who does this, his works will follow him. He may not be a hero to the world but he is one of God's heroes.

Canon Fredric Farrar

FREDRIC FARRAR (1831-1903)
Cleric of the Church of England and author.

APRIL 27

Some people are making such thorough preparation for rainy days that they aren't enjoying today's sunshine.

William Feather

WILLIAM FEATHER (1889-1981) American publisher and author.

APRIL 28

I believe in the sun, even when
    it is not shining.
I believe in love, even when
    feeling it not.
I believe in God, even when He
    is silent.

Louis Binstock

LOUIS BINSTOCK (1895-1974)
Rabbi of Temple of Sholom in
Chicago, Illinois. The quote was
originally written by a survivor
of the Holocaust on the wall of a
cell in Cologne.

APRIL 29

Inner sunshine warms not only the heart of the owner, but all who come in contact with it.

J. T. Fields

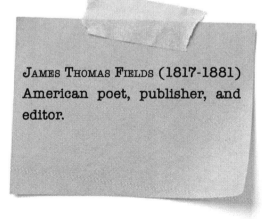

JAMES THOMAS FIELDS (1817-1881) American poet, publisher, and editor.

Wisdom for
Each Day

APRIL 30

The most glorious moments
in your life are not the
so-called days of success,
but rather those days
when out of dejection and
despair you feel rise in
you a challenge to life, and
the promise of the future
accomplishment.

Gustave Flaubert

GUSTAVE FLAUBERT (1821-1880)
French novelist.

MAY 1

Time deals gently only with those who take it gently.

Anatole France

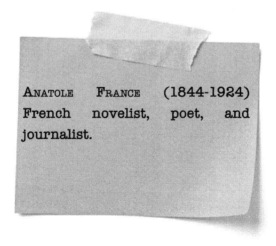

ANATOLE FRANCE (1844-1924) French novelist, poet, and journalist.

Wisdom for
Each Day

MAY 2

There is no pillow so soft
as a clear conscience.

French Proverb

~

Words of wisdom from
French antiquity.

~

MAY 3

If principle is good for anything, it is worth living up to.

Benjamin Franklin

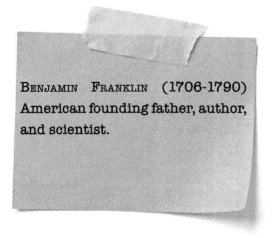

BENJAMIN FRANKLIN (1706-1790) American founding father, author, and scientist.

MAY 4

The world is full of willing
people: Some willing to
work, and the rest willing
to let them.

Robert Frost

ROBERT FROST (1874-1963)
American poet.

MAY 5

Courage is the human virtue that counts most-- courage to act on limited knowledge and insufficient evidence. That's all any of us have.

Robert Frost

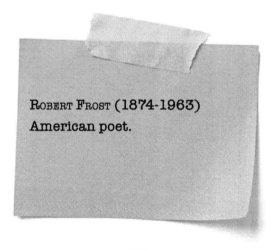

ROBERT FROST (1874-1963)
American poet.

MAY 6

Human improvement is from within outward.

James Anthony Froude

JAMES ANTHONY FROUDE
(1818-1894)
British historian.

MAY 7

You cannot teach a man anything; you can only help him to find it within himself.

Galileo

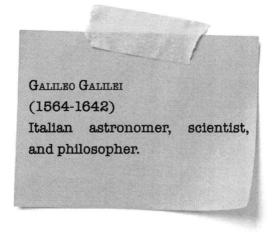

GALILEO GALILEI
(1564-1642)
Italian astronomer, scientist, and philosopher.

MAY 8

You must not lose faith in humanity. Humanity is an ocean; if a few drops of the ocean are dirty, the ocean does not become dirty.

Mahatma Gandhi

MAHATMA GANDHI
(1869-1948)
Leader of the Indian independence movement against colonial British rule.

MAY 9

Never give advice unless asked.

German Proverb

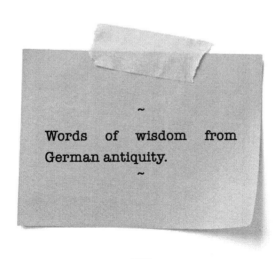

~

Words of wisdom from German antiquity.

~

Wisdom for
Each Day

MAY 10

God could not be everywhere,
and, therefore, he made
mothers.

Jewish Proverb

~

Words of wisdom from
Jewish antiquity.

~

MAY 11

God is the giver; stewardship
of what he gives is our
responsibility.

A.N. Gershom

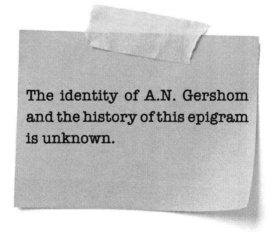

The identity of A.N. Gershom
and the history of this epigram
is unknown.

Wisdom for
Each Day

MAY 12

You pray in your distress and in your need; would that you might pray also in the fullness of your joy and in your days of abundance.

Kahlil Gibran

KAHLIL GIBRAN (1883-1931) Lebanese poet and writer.

MAY 13

You give but little when you give of your possessions. It is when you give of yourself that you truly give.

Kahlil Gibran

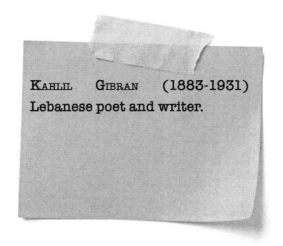

KAHLIL GIBRAN (1883-1931) Lebanese poet and writer.

MAY 14

Anger is never without a
reason but seldom with a
good one.

Benjamin Franklin

BENJAMIN FRANKLIN (1706-1790)
American founding father,
author, and scientist.

MAY 15

Correction does much, but encouragement does more. Encouragement after censure is as the sun after a shower.

Johann Wolfgang von Goethe

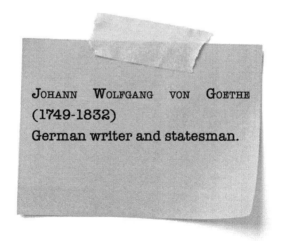

JOHANN WOLFGANG VON GOETHE (1749-1832)
German writer and statesman.

Wisdom for
Each Day

MAY 16

Life is the childhood of our
immortality.

Johann Wolfgang von Goethe

JOHANN WOLFGANG VON GOETHE
(1749-1832)
German writer and statesman.

MAY 17

Men show their character in nothing more clearly than by what they find laughable.

Johann Wolfgang von Goethe

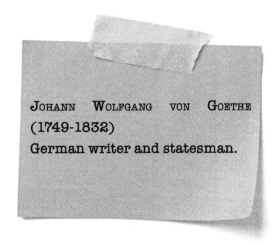

JOHANN WOLFGANG VON GOETHE (1749-1832)
German writer and statesman.

Wisdom for
Each Day

MAY 18

It is better to sleep on
what you intend doing than
to stay awake over what
you have done.

Anonymous

This anonymous saying was
printed in the Virginia Farm
Bureau News on August 1, 1964.

MAY 19

Beautiful young people are accidents of nature. But beautiful old people are works of art.

Marjorie Barstow Greenbie

MARJORIE BARSTOW GREENBIE
(1892-1976)
American author, historian, and women's rights activist.

MAY 20

I expect to pass through this world but once. Any good, therefore, that I can do, or any kindness that I can show to any fellow creature, let me do it now. Let me not defer it or neglect it, for I shall not pass this way again.

Stephen Grellet

STEPHEN GRELLET (1773-1855) French-born American Quaker missionary.

MAY 21

Real joy comes not from ease or riches or from the praise of men, but from doing something worthwhile.

Sir Wilfred Grenfell

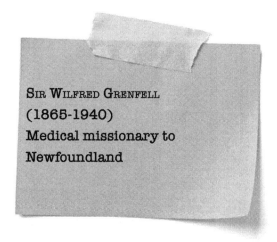

SIR WILFRED GRENFELL
(1865-1940)
Medical missionary to
Newfoundland

Wisdom for
Each Day

MAY 22

Let me be a little kinder
Let me be a little blinder
To the faults of those
around me.

Edgar A. Guest

EDGAR A. GUEST (1881-1959)
British-born American poet.

MAY 23

He started to sing as he
tackled the thing
That couldn't be done, and
he did it.

Edgar A. Guest

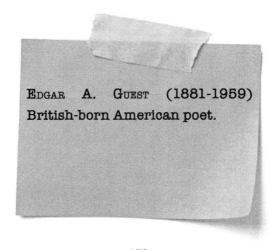

EDGAR A. GUEST (1881-1959)
British-born American poet.

Wisdom for
Each Day

MAY 24

That which is often asked of
God is not so much his will
and way as his approval of
our way.

Guideposts Magazine

GUIDEPOSTS MAGAZINE
Founded by Norman Vincent
Peale and his wife in 1945.

MAY 25

No mane in daily life ought to be satisfied with what his life now is. He ought every day to be looking forward to some of the possible improvements.

E.E. Hale

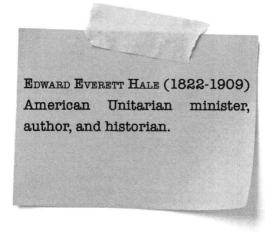

EDWARD EVERETT HALE (1822-1909) American Unitarian minister, author, and historian.

MAY 26

An audience of even one
gives us an opportunity
for a Christian witness.

A.Z. Hall

The identity of A.Z. Hall and
the history of this epigram is
unknown.

MAY 27

Faith is the substance
of things hoped for, the
evidence of things not seen.

Hebrews 11:1

KING JAMES VERSION, HOLY BIBLE
The King James Bible was issued
in 1611 by King James I and
became the official Christian
Bible for the Church of England.

Wisdom for
Each Day

MAY 28

Never a tear bedims the eye
that time and patience will
not dry.

Francis Bret Harte

FRANCIS BRET HARTE (1836-1902)
American writer.

MAY 29

For every evil under the sun
There is a remedy,
or there is none;
If there be one,
try and find it,
If there be none,
never mind it.

W.C. Hazlitt

WILLIAM CAREW HAZLITT (1834-1913)
British lawyer, writer, and editor.

MAY 30

And they who for their country die
Shall fill an honored grave,
For glory light the soldier's tomb,
And beauty weeps the brave.

J. R. Drake

JOSEPH RODMAN DRAKE (1795-1820)
Early American poet.

MAY 31

He that is good for making
excuses is seldom good for
anything else.

Benjamin Franklin

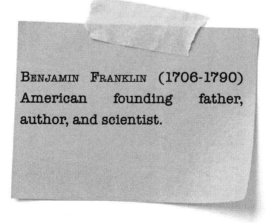

BENJAMIN FRANKLIN (1706-1790)
American founding father,
author, and scientist.

JUNE 1

A merry heart doeth good
like a medicine but a broken
spirit drieth the bones.

Proverbs 17:22

KING JAMES VERSION, HOLY BIBLE
The King James Bible was issued
in 1611 by King James I and
became the official Christian
Bible for the Church of England.

Wisdom for
Each Day

JUNE 2

For God is not unrighteous to forget your work and labor of love, which ye have shewed toward his name.

Hebrews 6:10

KING JAMES VERSION, HOLY BIBLE
The King James Bible was issued in 1611 by King James I and became the official Christian Bible for the Church of England.

JUNE 3

Jesus Christ the same yesterday, and today, and forever.

Hebrews 13:8

KING JAMES VERSION, HOLY BIBLE
The King James Bible was issued in 1611 by King James I and became the official Christian Bible for the Church of England.

Wisdom for
Each Day

JUNE 4

A wise man cares not for
what he cannot have.

George Herbert

GEORGE HERBERT (1593-1633)
Welsh poet and Anglican priest.

JUNE 5

'Tis a lesson you should heed;
Try, Try, Try again,
If at first you don't succeed,
Try, Try, Try again.

W. E. Hickson

WILLIAM EDWARD HICKSON
(1803-1870)
British educational writer.

Wisdom for
Each Day

JUNE 6

No one can disgrace us but ourselves.

J.G. Holland

JOSIAH GILBERT HOLLAND
(1819-1881)
American novelist and poet.

JUNE 7

The mind that is cheerful at present will have solicitude for the future and will meet the bitter occurrences of life with a smile.

Horace

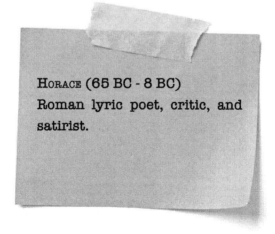

HORACE (65 BC - 8 BC)
Roman lyric poet, critic, and satirist.

JUNE 8

Kind hearts are the gardens,
Kind thoughts are the roots,
Kind words are the flowers,
Kind deeds are the fruits.

Henry Wadsworth Longfellow

HENRY WADSWORTH LONGFELLOW
(1856-1915)
American poet, artist, and
philosopher.

JUNE 9

Every man is a fool for at least five minutes every day. Wisdom consists in not exceeding the limit.

Elbert Hubbard

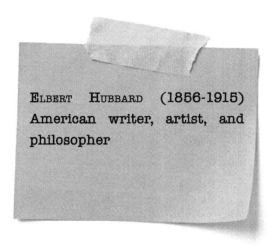

ELBERT HUBBARD (1856-1915) American writer, artist, and philosopher

Wisdom for
Each Day

June 10

Patience and gentleness is
power.

Leigh Hunt

LEIGH HUNT (1784-1859)
British critic, essayist, and poet.

JUNE 11

It is not who is right, but what is right, that is important.

Thomas Henry Huxley

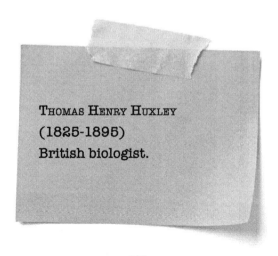

THOMAS HENRY HUXLEY
(1825-1895)
British biologist.

Wisdom for
Each Day

JUNE 12

My creed is this:
   Happiness is only good,
   The place to be happy is here
   The time to be happy is now
   The way to be happy is to
   Make others so.

                    Robert G. Ingersoll

ROBERT GREEN INGERSOLL
(1833-1899)
American lawyer and Civil War
Veteran.

JUNE 13

They that wait upon the
Lord shall renew their
strength.

Isaiah 40:31

KING JAMES VERSION, HOLY BIBLE
The King James Bible was issued
in 1611 by King James I and
became the official Christian
Bible for the Church of England.

Wisdom for
Each Day

JUNE 14

The grass withers, the
flower fades; but the word
of our God will stand for
ever.

Isaiah 40:8

REVISED STANDARD VERSION,
HOLY BIBLE
The Revised Standard Version
was printed in 1901 to revise
the King James Bible.

June 15

Let the beauty of Jesus be
seen in me.

                    Noel Jayahan

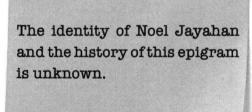

The identity of Noel Jayahan
and the history of this epigram
is unknown.

Wisdom for
Each Day

JUNE 16

Happiness grows at our own firesides, and is not to be picked in strangers' gardens.

Douglas Jerrold

DOUGLAS JERROLD (1803-1857) British playwright and journalist.

JUNE 17

Blessed are they that have
not seen and yet have
believed.

John 20:29

KING JAMES VERSION, HOLY BIBLE
The King James Bible was issued
in 1611 by King James I and
became the official Christian
Bible for the Church of England.

Wisdom for
Each Day

JUNE 18

Many individuals have, like
uncut diamonds, shining
qualities beneath a tough
exterior.

Juvenal

DECIMUS JUNIUS JUVENAL (c.55-127)
Roman satiric poet.

JUNE 19

God is love: and he that
dwelleth in love dwelleth
in God, and God in him.

1 John 4:16

KING JAMES VERSION, HOLY BIBLE
The King James Bible was issued
in 1611 by King James I and
became the official Christian
Bible for the Church of England.

JUNE 20

He who waits to do a great
deal of good at once, will
never do anything.

Samuel Johnson

SAMUEL JOHNSON (1709-1784)
British poet, essayist, and critic.

June 21

Every man has three characters: That which he exhibits, that which he has, and that which he thinks he has.

Jean-Baptiste Alphonse Karr

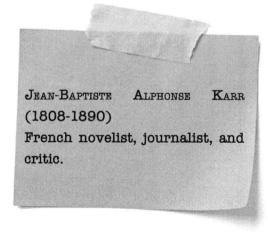

JEAN-BAPTISTE ALPHONSE KARR (1808-1890)
French novelist, journalist, and critic.

JUNE 22

Keep your face to the sunshine and you cannot see the shadow.

Helen Keller

HELEN KELLER (1880-1968)
Blind and deaf American author and educator.

JUNE 23

Face your deficiencies and acknowledge them, but do not let them master you. Let them teach you patience, sweetness, insight. When we do the best we can, we never know what miracle is wrought in our own life, or in the life of another.

Helen Keller

HELEN KELLER (1880-1968)
Blind and deaf American author and educator.

June 24

I kneel not now to pray that thou
Make white one single sin,
I only kneel to thank thee, Lord,
For what I have not been.

Harry Kemp

HARRY KEMP (1883-1960)
American poet and prose
writer.

JUNE 25

Constantly choose rather to want less, than to have more.

Thomas a' Kempis

THOMAS A' KEMPIS (1380-1471) German Christian theologian and author of The Imitation of Christ.

Wisdom for
Each Day

June 26

Thou wilt always rejoice
in the evening if thou has
spent the day profitable.

Thomas a' Kempis

THOMAS A' KEMPIS (1380-1471)
German Christian theologian
and author of The Imitation of
Christ.

JUNE 27

Endeavor to be patient in bearing with the defects and infirmities of others, of what sort so ever they be; for that thyself also hast many failings which must be borned with by others.

Thomas a'Kempis

THOMAS A' KEMPIS (1380-1471) German Christian theologian and author of The Imitation of Christ.

Wisdom for
Each Day

JUNE 28

Life can be only understood
backward, but it must be
lived forward.

Søren Kierkegaard

SØREN KIERKEGAARD (1813-1855)
Danish theologian, poet, and
existential philosopher.

JUNE 29

We act as though comfort and luxury were the chief requirements of life, when all that we need to make us happy is something to be enthusiastic about.

Charles Kingsley

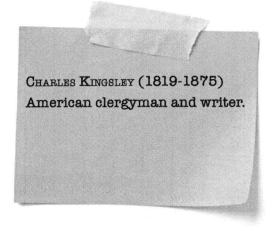

CHARLES KINGSLEY (1819-1875)
American clergyman and writer.

June 30

There are two ways to slide easily through life: To believe everything or to doubt everything. Both ways save us from thinking.

Alfred Korzybski

ALFRED KORZYBSKI (1879-1950) Polish-American scholar.

JULY 1

It is easier to be wise for others than for ourselves.

François de La Rouchefoucauld

FRANÇOIS DE LA ROUCHEFOUCAULD (1613-1680)
French writer.

July 2

Whatever your lot in life,
build something on it.

Home Life

The exact magazine and
history of this epigram is
unknown.

JULY 3

Everybody   has   to   be
somebody to somebody to be
anybody.

Malcom Forbes

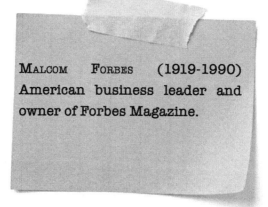

MALCOM   FORBES   (1919-1990)
American business leader and
owner of Forbes Magazine.

Wisdom for
Each Day

JULY 4

I realize that patriotism
is not enough. I must have
no hatred toward anyone.

Edith Cavell

EDITH CAVELL (1865-1915)
British nurse and heroine during
World War I.

July 5

It is a great misfortune
neither to have enough wit
to talk well nor enough
judgment to be silent.

Jean de la Bruyère

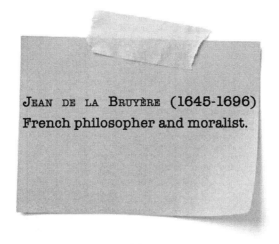

JEAN DE LA BRUYÈRE (1645-1696)
French philosopher and moralist.

July 6

Work is the easiest way man has ever invented to escape boredom.

De Recueil

This quotation was printed in the Palmyra Spectator newspaper in Missouri on August 18, 1955.

JULY 7

If only one could have two
lives; the first in which to
make one's mistakes, and the
second in which to profit
by them.

D.H. Lawrence

DAVID HERBERT LAWRENCE
(1885-1930)
British novelist, poet, and
playwright.

Wisdom for
Each Day

JULY 8

No mariner every enters upon a more uncharted sea than does the average human being born in the 20th century. Our ancestors knew their way from birth through eternity; we are puzzled about the day after tomorrow.

Walter Lippman

WALTER LIPPMAN (1889-1974)
American newspaper commentator and author.

JULY 9

You can fool some of the people all of the time, and all of the people some of the time, but you cannot fool all of the people all of the time.

Abraham Lincoln

ABRAHAM LINCOLN (1809-1865) 16th President of the United States.

Wisdom for
Each Day

July 10

Not in the clamor of the crowded street,
Not in the shouts and plaudits of the throng,
But in ourselves, are triumph and defeat.

Henry Wadsworth Longfellow

HENRY WADSWORTH LONGFELLOW (1856-1915)
American poet, artist, and philosopher.

JULY 11

We judge ourselves by what
we feel capable of doing,
while others judge us by
what we have already done.

Henry Wadsworth Longfellow

HENRY WADSWORTH LONGFELLOW
(1856-1915)
American poet, artist, and
philosopher.

Wisdom for
Each Day

JULY 12

Not what we give, but what we share
For the gift without the giver is bare.

J.R. Lowell

JAMES RUSSELL LOWELL (1819-1891)
American Romantic poet and
critic.

July 13

Be still, sad heart! And cease
repining;
Behind the clouds is the sun
still shining.

Henry Wadsworth Longfellow

HENRY WADSWORTH LONGFELLOW
(1856-1915)
American poet, artist, and
philosopher.

July 14

Blessed are they who have nothing to say, and cannot be persuaded to say it.

J.R. Lowell

JAMES RUSSELL LOWELL (1819-1891) American Romantic poet and critic.

JULY 15

Let us be of good cheer, remembering that the misfortunes hardest to bear are those which never happen.

J.R. Lowell

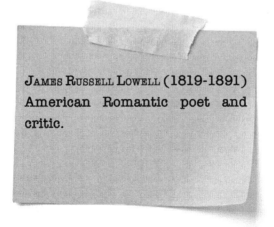

JAMES RUSSELL LOWELL (1819-1891) American Romantic poet and critic.

JULY 16

The only gracious way to accept an insult is to ignore it. If you can't ignore it, top it. If you can't top it, laugh at it. If you can't laugh at it, it's probably deserved.

Russell Lynes

RUSSELL LYNES (1910-1991) American art historian and author.

July 17

Worry is the interest paid by those who borrow trouble.

George W. Lyon

This epigram by George W. Lyon was printed in the Harrisburg Telegraph in Pennsylvania on January 30, 1937.

JULY 18

Everyone must have felt that a cheerful friend is like a sunny day, which sheds its brightness on all around; and most of us can, as we choose, make of this world either a palace or a prison.

Sir John Lubbock

SIR JOHN LUBBOCK (1834-1913) British banker, politician, and philanthropist.

JULY 19

Not my will, but thine be done.

Luke 22:42

KING JAMES VERSION, HOLY BIBLE
The King James Bible was issued in 1611 by King James I and became the official Christian Bible for the Church of England.

JULY 20

All anyone ever has is today because yesterday is gone and tomorrow never comes.

Douglas Lurton

DOUGLAS LURTON (dates unknown) Author of Power of Positive Thinking, published in 1950.

JULY 21

God writes the gospel not in the Bible alone, but on trees and flowers, and clouds, and stars.

Martin Luther

MARTIN LUTHER (1483-1546) German theologian responsible for the Protestant Reformation.

JULY 22

There is no security on this earth. There is only opportunity.

General Douglas MacArthur

GENERAL DOUGLAS MACARTHUR (1880-1964) U.S. general and commander of the Southwest Pacific Theater in World War II.

JULY 23

Decide promptly, but never give any reasons. Your decisions may be right, but your reasons are sure to be wrong.

William Murray,
Earl of Mansfield

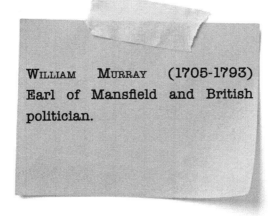

WILLIAM MURRAY (1705-1793) Earl of Mansfield and British politician.

JULY 24

Make it a rule of life
never to regret and never
to look back. Regret is an
appalling waste of energy;
you can't build on it; it's
only good for wallowing in.

Katherine Mansfield

KATHERINE MANSFIELD (1888-1923)
Pen name for Kathleen Mansfield
Murry, New Zealand born author.

JULY 25

That which is good to be
done cannot be done too
soon; and if it is neglected
to be done early, it will
frequently happen that it
will not be done at all.

Bishop Richard Mant

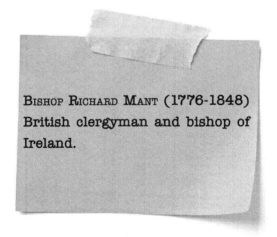

BISHOP RICHARD MANT (1776-1848)
British clergyman and bishop of
Ireland.

July 26

Christianity taught men that love is worth more than intelligence.

Jacques Maritain

JACQUES MARITAIN (1882-1973) Roman Catholic philosopher.

JULY 27

Love has the power of
making you believe what
you would normally treat
with the deepest suspicion.

Pierre Marivaux

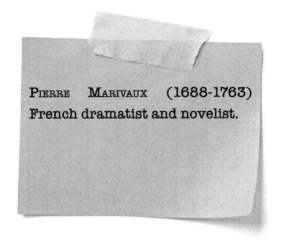

PIERRE MARIVAUX (1688-1763)
French dramatist and novelist.

Wisdom for
Each Day

July 28

All things are possible to
him that believeth.

Mark 9:23

KING JAMES VERSION, HOLY BIBLE
The King James Bible was issued
in 1611 by King James I and
became the official Christian
Bible for the Church of England.

July 29

Lord, when we are wrong,
make us willing to change.
And when we are right, make
us easy to live with.

Peter Marshall

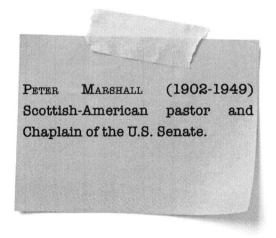

PETER MARSHALL (1902-1949)
Scottish-American pastor and
Chaplain of the U.S. Senate.

Wisdom for
Each Day

JULY 30

If you would be loved, love
and be lovable.

Benjamin Franklin

BENJAMIN FRANKLIN (1706-1790)
American founding father,
author, and scientist.

JULY 31

The unfortunate thing about this world is that good habits are so much easier to get out of than bad ones.

Somerset Maugham

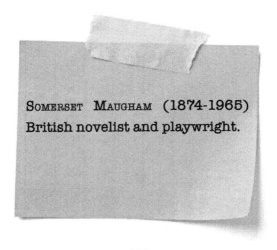

SOMERSET MAUGHAM (1874-1965)
British novelist and playwright.

AUGUST 1

Therefore, do not be anxious about tomorrow, for tomorrow will be anxious for itself. Let the day's own trouble be sufficient for the day.

Mathew 4:10

REVISED STANDARD VERSION, HOLY BIBLE
The Revised Standard Version was printed in 1901 to revise the King James Bible.

AUGUST 2

Every one that asketh
receiveth, and he that
seeketh findeth.

Mathew 7:8

KING JAMES VERSION, HOLY BIBLE
The King James Bible was issued
in 1611 by King James I and
became the official Christian
Bible for the Church of England.

AUGUST 3

The greatest happiness of
life is the conviction that
we are loved; loved for
ourselves, or rather, loved
in spite of ourselves.

Victor Hugo

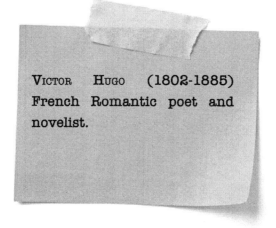

VICTOR HUGO (1802-1885)
French Romantic poet and
novelist.

August 4

What is a man profited, if he shall gain the whole world and lose his own soul.

Mathew 16:26

KING JAMES VERSION, HOLY BIBLE
The King James Bible was issued in 1611 by King James I and became the official Christian Bible for the Church of England.

AUGUST 5

Trouble is the structural steel that goes into the building of character.

Douglas Meador

BEN DOUGLAS MEADOR (1901-1974)
Texan journalist.

AUGUST 6

If it's very painful for you to criticize your friends, you're safe in doing it. But if you take the slightest pleasure in it, that's the time to hold your tongue.

Alice Duer Miller

ALICE DUER MILLER (1874-1942) American poet and suffragist.

August 7

Lord, grant that I may always desire more than I accomplish.

Michealangelo

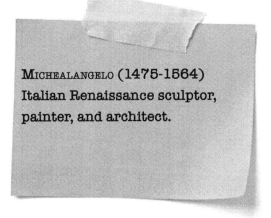

Michealangelo (1475-1564)
Italian Renaissance sculptor, painter, and architect.

Wisdom for
Each Day

AUGUST 8

A man's true wealth is the
good he does in this world.

Mohammad

MOHAMMAD (c. 570-632)
Founder of Islam.

258

AUGUST 9

It is not alone what we do, but also what we do not do, for which we are accountable.

Molière

MOLIÈRE (1622-1673)
Known also as Jean-Baptiste Poquelin, French comedic playwright and actor.

AUGUST 10

Verily I say unto you, inasmuch as ye have done it unto one of the least of these my breathen, ye have done it unto me.

Mathew 25:40

KING JAMES VERSION, HOLY BIBLE
The King James Bible was issued in 1611 by King James I and became the official Christian Bible for the Church of England.

August 11

The less men think, the more they talk.

Montesquieu

Montesquieu (1689-1755) French lawyer and political philosopher during the Enlightenment.

Wisdom for
Each Day

AUGUST 12

If you treat a man as he is,
he will stay as he is, but
if you treat him as if he
were what he ought to be,
and could be, he will become
that bigger and better man.

Johann Wolfgang von Goethe

JOHANN WOLFGANG VON GOETHE
(1749-1832)
German writer and statesman.

AUGUST 13

Neither do men light a candle and put it under a bushel, but on a candlestick, and it giveth light unto all that are in the house.

Mathew 5:15

KING JAMES VERSION, HOLY BIBLE
The King James Bible was issued in 1611 by King James I and became the official Christian Bible for the Church of England.

Wisdom for
Each Day

AUGUST 14

A man travels the world
over in search of what he
needs and returns home to
find it.

George Moore

GEORGE AUGUSTUS MOORE
(1852-1933)
Irish writer and poet.

AUGUST 15

There is no surprise the more magical that the surprise of being loved. It is the finger of God on a man's shoulder.

Charles Morgan

CHARLES MORGAN (1894-1958) British novelist and playwright.

AUGUST 16

The world is divided into
people who do things and
people who get the credit.
Try, if you can, to belong
to the first class. There's
far less competition.

Dwight Morrow

DWIGHT MORROW (1873-1931)
American businessman and
politician.

August 17

This day I will become part of the Life of someone who needs help.

D. H. Mundt

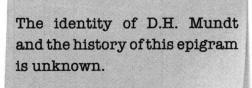

The identity of D.H. Mundt and the history of this epigram is unknown.

Wisdom for
Each Day

AUGUST 18

Examinations are formidable
even to the best prepared,
for the greatest fool may
ask more than the wisest
man can answer.

Charles Caleb Colton

CHARLES CALEB COLTON (1780-1832)
British cleric and writer.

AUGUST 19

Whatever you ask in prayer
you will receive, if you
have faith.

Mathew 21:22

REVISED STANDARD VERSION,
HOLY BIBLE
The Revised Standard Version
was printed in 1901 to revise the
King James Bible.

Wisdom for
Each Day

AUGUST 20

The kindness planned for tomorrow doesn't count today.

Newark (Del.) Post

This saying (and the accompanying citation) was published in the Fort Lauderdale News on January 9, 1966.

August 21

There are two things that go into the make-up of friendship, the one is truth, the other is understanding.

Anonymous

The history of this anonymous saying is unknown.

Wisdom for
Each Day

AUGUST 22

The journey of a thousand miles begins with a single step.

Lao Tzu

LAO TZU (640 BC - 531 BC)
Chinese philosopher, writer, and founder of Taoism.

AUGUST 23

When a man has quietly made up his mind that there is nothing he cannot endure, his fears leave him.

Grove Patterson

GROVE PATTERSON
(dates unknown)
Editor of the Toledo Blaze newspaper from the mid-1900s.

AUGUST 24

The trouble with the most of us is that we would rather be ruined by praise than saved by criticism.

Norman Vincent Peale

NORMAN VINCENT PEALE
(1898-1993)
American clergyman.

AUGUST 25

Religion is nothing else but love to God and man.

William Penn

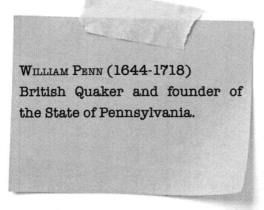

WILLIAM PENN (1644-1718)
British Quaker and founder of the State of Pennsylvania.

AUGUST 26

Love by its presence, like God by his, makes everything not necessarily clear or right or even good, but acceptable. Whereas in its absence, as in His, there is no hope.

Virgilia Peterson

VIRGILIA PETERSON (1904-1966) Polish-American writer and journalist.

AUGUST 27

We tire of those pleasures
we take, but never of those
we give.

John Petit-Senn

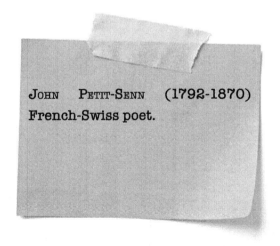

JOHN PETIT-SENN (1792-1870)
French-Swiss poet.

AUGUST 28

The man who makes no mistakes does not usually make anything.

Edward J. Phelps

EDWARD JOHN PHELPS (1822-1900)
American lawyer and diplomat.

August 29

A kind heart is a fountain of
gladness, making everything
in its vicinity freshen into
smiles.

Washington Irving

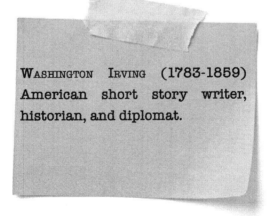

WASHINGTON IRVING (1783-1859)
American short story writer,
historian, and diplomat.

August 30

Hasten slowly.

Augustus Caesar

AUGUSTUS CAESAR (63 BC - 14 AD) emperor of Rome from 27 BC to 14 AD.

August 31

If the head and the body are to be well, you must begin by curing the soul.

Plato

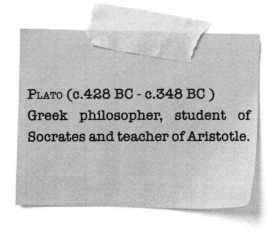

PLATO (c.428 BC - c.348 BC)
Greek philosopher, student of Socrates and teacher of Aristotle.

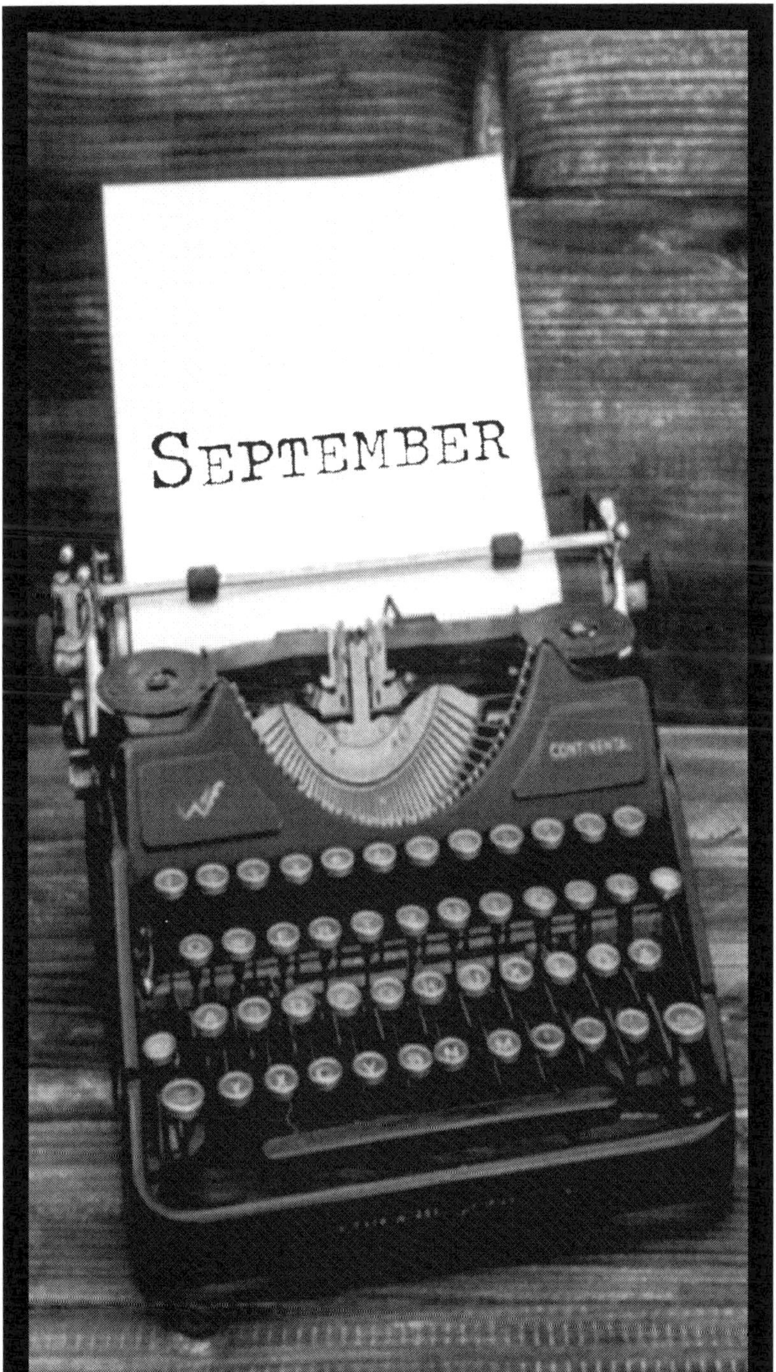
SEPTEMBER

SEPTEMBER 1

We can easily forgive a child who is afraid of the dark; the real tragedy of life is when men are afraid of the light.

Plato

PLATO (c.428 BC - c.348 BC)
Greek philosopher, student of Socrates and teacher of Aristotle.

SEPTEMBER 2

Good nature and good sense
must ever join;
To err is human, to forgive,
divine.

Alexander Pope,
Essay on Criticism

ALEXANDER POPE (1688-1744)
British poet and satirist.

SEPTEMBER 3

If I am right, thy grace impart,
Still in the right to stay;
If I am wrong, O teach my heart
To find that better way!

Alexander Pope,
Universal Prayer

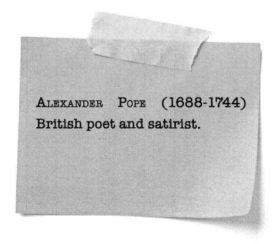

ALEXANDER POPE (1688-1744)
British poet and satirist.

SEPTEMBER 4

Lord, send me work to do for Thee,
Let not a single day
Be spent in waiting on myself,
Or wasted pass away.

Elizabeth Prentiss

ELIZABETH PRENTISS (1818-1878)
American religious writer and
hymn writer.

SEPTEMBER 5

Indecision is fatal. It is better to make a wrong decision than build up a habit of indecision.

Marie Beynon Ray

MARIE BEYNON RAY (1891-1969) American writer and editor of Vogue and Harper's Bazaar Magazines.

Wisdom for
Each Day

SEPTEMBER 6

Hours are golden links;
God's token, reaching
heaven; but, one by one
take them, lest the chain be
broken, ere the pilgrimage
be done.

Adelaid A. Proctor

ADELAID ANNE PROCTOR (1825-1864)
British poet and philantropist.

September 7

It is not easy to find happiness in ourselves, and it is not possible to find it elsewhere.

Agnes Repplier

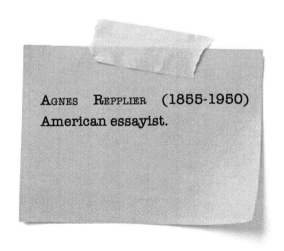

AGNES REPPLIER (1855-1950) American essayist.

SEPTEMBER 8

Trust in the Lord with all thine heart; and lean not unto thine own understanding.

Proverbs 3:5

KING JAMES VERSION, HOLY BIBLE
The King James Bible was issued in 1611 by King James I and became the official Christian Bible for the Church of England.

September 9

You can't hold a man down without staying down with him.

Booker T. Washington

Booker Taliaferro Washington (1856-1915)
American educator, reformer, and author.

September 10

Happy is the man that findeth wisdom and the man that getteth understanding.

Proverbs 3:13

KING JAMES VERSION, HOLY BIBLE
The King James Bible was issued in 1611 by King James I and became the official Christian Bible for the Church of England.

SEPTEMBER 11

I do not love him because
he is good, but because he
is my child.

Rabindranath Tagore

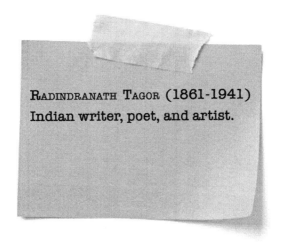

RADINDRANATH TAGOR (1861-1941)
Indian writer, poet, and artist.

SEPTEMBER 12

Don't let yesterday use up too much of today.

Will Rogers

WILL ROGERS (1879-1935) American entertainer and comedian.

SEPTEMBER 13

A soft answer turneth away wrath.

Proverbs 15:1

KING JAMES VERSION, HOLY BIBLE
The King James Bible was issued in 1611 by King James I and became the official Christian Bible for the Church of England.

SEPTEMBER 14

Disappointment   is   the
nurse of wisdom.

Sir Boyle Roche

Sir   Boyle   Roche (1736-1807)
Irish politician.

SEPTEMBER 15

This is the day which the
Lord hath made; we shall
rejoice and be glad in it.

Psalms 118:24

KING JAMES VERSION, HOLY BIBLE
The King James Bible was issued
in 1611 by King James I and
became the official Christian
Bible for the Church of England.

Wisdom for
Each Day

SEPTEMBER 16

In God have I put my trust;
I will not be afraid what
man can do unto me.

Psalms 56:11

KING JAMES VERSION, HOLY BIBLE
The King James Bible was issued
in 1611 by King James I and
became the official Christian
Bible for the Church of England.

September 17

The only thing we have to fear is fear itself.

Franklin D. Roosevelt

FRANKLIN DELANO ROOSEVELT
(1882-1945)
32nd President of the United States.

September 18

O give thanks unto the Lord, for he is good: For His mercy endureth forver.

Psalms 107:1

KING JAMES VERSION, HOLY BIBLE
The King James Bible was issued in 1611 by King James I and became the official Christian Bible for the Church of England.

SEPTEMBER 19

The cautious seldom err.

Confucius

CONFUCIUS (551 BC - 479 BC)
Chinese philosopher and political theorist, founder of Confucianism.

SEPTEMBER 20

God is our refuge and strength, a very present help in trouble.

Psalms 46:1

KING JAMES VERSION, HOLY BIBLE
The King James Bible was issued in 1611 by King James I and became the official Christian Bible for the Church of England.

September 21

The oldest, shortest words
— yes and no — are those
which require the most
thought.

Pythagorus

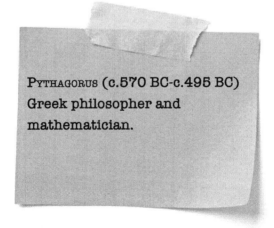

PYTHAGORUS (c.570 BC-c.495 BC)
Greek philosopher and
mathematician.

Wisdom for
Each Day

SEPTEMBER 22

The entire sum of existence
is the magic of being needed
by just one person.

Violet Putnam

VIOLET PUTNAM (1923-?)
Canadian writer.

SEPTEMBER 23

Wit is the salt of conversation, not the food.

William Hazlitt

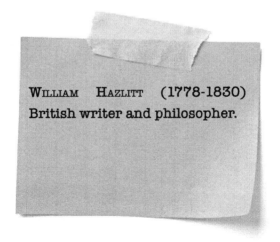

WILLIAM HAZLITT (1778-1830)
British writer and philosopher.

Wisdom for
Each Day

SEPTEMBER 24

If God be for us, who can be against us?

Romans 8:31

KING JAMES VERSION, HOLY BIBLE
The King James Bible was issued in 1611 by King James I and became the official Christian Bible for the Church of England.

SEPTEMBER 25

He who is the most slow in making a promise is the most faithful in the performance of it.

Jean-Jacques Rousseau

JEAN-JACQUES ROUSSEAU (1712-1778)
European philosopher and writer.

SEPTEMBER 26

Silences make the real conversations between friends. Not the saying but the never needing to say is what counts.

Margaret Lee Runbeck

MARGARET LEE RUNBECK
(1905-1956)
American author.

SEPTEMBER 27

He who sings frightens away his ills.

Miguel de Cervantes

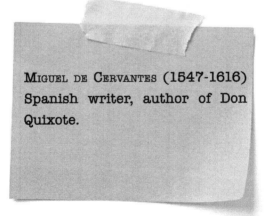

MIGUEL DE CERVANTES (1547-1616)
Spanish writer, author of Don Quixote.

SEPTEMBER 28

To be without some of the things you want is an indispensable part of happiness.

Bertrand Russell

BERTRAND RUSSELL (1872-1970) British philosopher, writer, political activist, and Nobel laureate.

SEPTEMBER 29

Mankind is divisible into
two great classes: hosts,
and guests.

Sir "Max" Henry Beerbohm

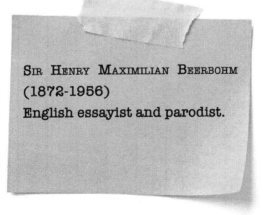

SIR HENRY MAXIMILIAN BEERBOHM
(1872-1956)
English essayist and parodist.

Wisdom for
Each Day

September 30

Faith is to believe what we do not see; and the reward of this faith is to see what we believe.

Saint Augustine

SAINT AUGUSTINE (354-430)
Bishop of Hippo from 396 to 430.

OCTOBER 1

The test of a preacher is that his congregation goes away saying not, "What a lovely sermon," but "I will do something."

Saint Francis de Sales

SAINT FRANCIS DE SALES
(1567-1622)
Bishop of Geneva and saint in the Catholic Church.

OCTOBER 2

Life is like an onion; you peel it off one layer at a time, and sometimes you weep.

Carl Sandburg

CARL SANDBURG (1878-1967) Swedish-American poet and writer, winner of three Pulitzer Prizes.

OCTOBER 3

Those who cannot remember
the past are condemned to
repeat it.

George Santayana

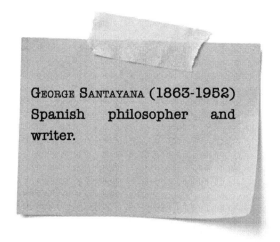

GEORGE SANTAYANA (1863-1952)
Spanish philosopher and
writer.

Wisdom for
Each Day

OCTOBER 4

Happiness is like a kiss;
You must share it to have
it.

Olivio Santoro

OLIVIO SANTORO (1928-?)
Child musician and yodler from
Long Island.

October 5

Only those who have the patience to do simple things perfectly ever acquire the skill to do difficult things easily.

Johann Friedrich von Schiller

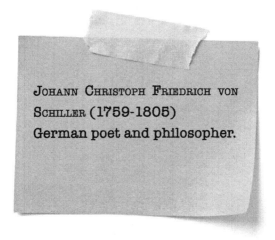

JOHANN CHRISTOPH FRIEDRICH VON SCHILLER (1759-1805)
German poet and philosopher.

OCTOBER 6

Disappointments are to the soul what a thunderstorm is to the air.

Johann Friedrich von Schiller

JOHANN CHRISTOPH FRIEDRICH VON SCHILLER (1759-1805)
German poet and philosopher.

OCTOBER 7

An open door of opportunity can be God's way of speaking to me today.

Anonymous

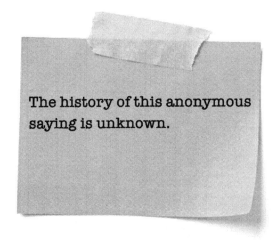

The history of this anonymous saying is unknown.

OCTOBER 8

If you have built castles in the air, your work need not be lost; that is where they should be. Now put the foundations under them.

Henry Thoreau

HENR DAVID THOREAU (1817-1862)
American writer, abolitionist, and philosopher.

OCTOBER 9

Begin at once to live, and count each day as a separate life.

Lucius Annaeus Seneca

LUCIUS ANNAEUS SENECA
(4 BC - 65 AD)
Roman Stoic philosopher and statesman.

Wisdom for
Each Day

OCTOBER 10

He who gives to me, teaches
me to give.

Danish Proverb

~

Words of wisdom from
Danish antiquity.

~

OCTOBER 11

Be master of your petty annoyances and conserve your energies for the big, worthwhile things. It isn't the mountain ahead that wears you out — it's the grain of sand in your shoe.

Robert Service

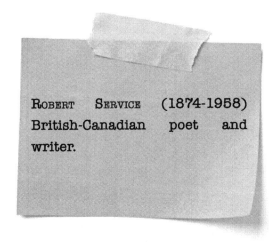

ROBERT SERVICE (1874-1958) British-Canadian poet and writer.

Wisdom for
Each Day

OCTOBER 12

To thine own self be true,
And it must follow as the
night the day
Thou canst not then be
false to any man.

William Shakespeare

WILLIAM SHAKESPEARE (1564- 1616)
Elizabethan poet and playwright.

OCTOBER 13

The less we know, the more
we suspect.

Henry Wheeler Shaw

HENRY WHEELER SHAW (1818-1885)
Pen name for Josh Billings:
American humorist, writer, and
lecturer.

OCTOBER 14

We have no more right to consume happiness without producing it than to consume wealth without producing it.

George Bernard Shaw

GEORGE BERNARD SHAW (1856-1950)
Irish playwright and critic.

OCTOBER 15

The best place to seek God is in the garden. You can dig for Him there.

George Bernard Shaw

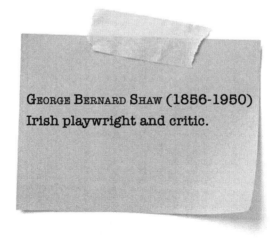

GEORGE BERNARD SHAW (1856-1950)
Irish playwright and critic.

OCTOBER 16

Religion is a great force —
the only real motive force
in the world; but your must
get at a man through his
own religion, not through
yours.

George Bernard Shaw

GEORGE BERNARD SHAW (1856-1950)
Irish playwright and critic.

OCTOBER 17

Have more than thou showest; Speak less than thou knowest.

William Shakespeare

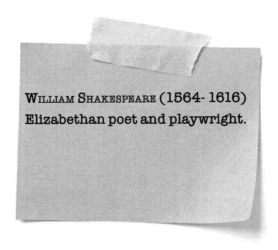

WILLIAM SHAKESPEARE (1564- 1616)
Elizabethan poet and playwright.

OCTOBER 18

The happiest miser on earth — the man who saves up every friend he can make.

Robert E. Sherwood

ROBERT EMMET SHERWOOD
(1896-1955)
American playwright and screenwriter.

OCTOBER 19

Pray as if everything depended on God, and work as if everything depended upon man.

Cardinal Francis Spellman

FRANCIS SPELLMAN (1889-1967) American bishop and cardinal of the Catholic Church.

OCTOBER 20

The shortest and surest way
to live with honor in the
world is to be in reality
what we appear to be.

Socrates

SOCRATES (c.470 BC - 399 BC)
Greek philosopher considered
the founder of Western
philosophy.

OCTOBER 21

If all of our misfortunes were laid in one common heap, whence everyone must take an equal portion, most people would be contented to take their own and depart.

Socrates

SOCRATES (c.470 BC - 399 BC) Greek philosopher considered the founder of Western philosophy.

Wisdom for
Each Day

OCTOBER 22

Our prayers should be for
blessings in general, for
God knows best what is good
for us.

Socrates

SOCRATES (c.470 BC - 399 BC)
Greek philosopher considered
the founder of Western
philosophy.

OCTOBER 23

Pleasure is very reflective,
and if you give it you will
feel it.

Sydney Smith

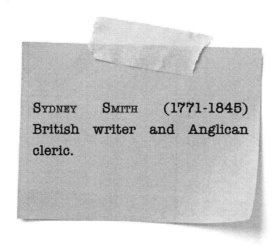

SYDNEY SMITH (1771-1845)
British writer and Anglican
cleric.

Wisdom for
Each Day

OCTOBER 24

Keep your fears to yourself,
but share your courage
with others.

Robert Louis Stevenson

ROBERT LOUIS STEVENSON
(1850-1894)
Scottish novelist and poet.

OCTOBER 25

Anyone can carry his burden, however hard, until nightfall. Anyone can do his work, however hard, for one day. And this is all that life really means.

Robert Louis Stevenson

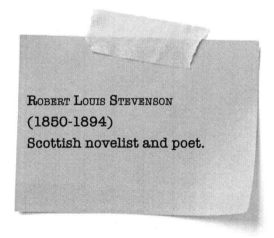

ROBERT LOUIS STEVENSON
(1850-1894)
Scottish novelist and poet.

October 26

Faith is the key to fit the door called Hope, but there is no power anywhere, Like Love, for turning it.

Elaine V. Emans

ELAINE V. EMANS (dates unknown) Mid-1900s writer and poet.

October 27

The saints are the sinners
who keep on trying.

Robert Louis Stevenson

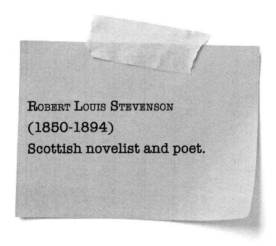

ROBERT LOUIS STEVENSON
(1850-1894)
Scottish novelist and poet.

Wisdom for
Each Day

OCTOBER 28

To work is to worship, to be cheery is to pray, to be happy is the first step towards being pious.

Robert Louis Stevenson

ROBERT LOUIS STEVENSON
(1850-1894)
Scottish novelist and poet.

October 29

God is always with us — no
matter what happens.

J.K. Stickney, Jr.

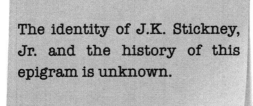

The identity of J.K. Stickney,
Jr. and the history of this
epigram is unknown.

OCTOBER 30

I regret often that I have spoken, never that I have been silent.

Pubilius Syrus

PUBILIUS SYRUS (85 BC - c. 43 BC)
Latin writer born in Syria.

October 31

Many receive advice, only the wise profit by it.

Pubilius Syrus

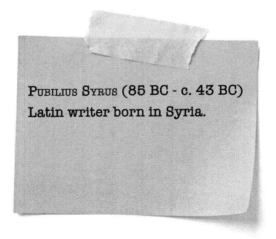

Pubilius Syrus (85 BC - c. 43 BC)
Latin writer born in Syria.

NOVEMBER 1

If you wish to reach the
highest, begin at the lowest.

Pubilius Syrus

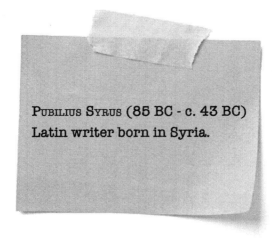

PUBILIUS SYRUS (85 BC - c. 43 BC)
Latin writer born in Syria.

Wisdom for
Each Day

NOVEMBER 2

The circumstances of others
seem good to us, while ours
seems good to others.

Pubilius Syrus

PUBILIUS SYRUS (85 BC - c. 43 BC)
Latin writer born in Syria.

November 3

Although men are accused of not knowing their own weakness, yet perhaps as few know their own strength. It is in man as in soils, where sometimes there is a vein of gold which the owner knows not of.

Jonathan Swift

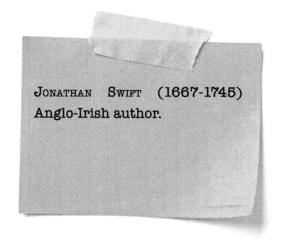

JONATHAN SWIFT (1667-1745)
Anglo-Irish author.

NOVEMBER 4

Fame is what you have taken,
Character's what you give;
When to this truth you waken,
Then you begin to live.

Bayard Taylor

BAYARD TAYLOR (1825-1878)
American author and poet.

NOVEMBER 5

Faith is the bird that feels the light and sings when the dawn is still dark.

Rabindranath Tagore

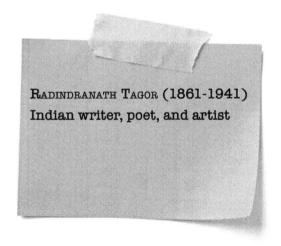

RADINDRANATH TAGOR (1861-1941)
Indian writer, poet, and artist

November 6

A good laugh is sunshine in a house.

William Thackeray

WILLIAM MAKEPEACE THACKERAY (1811-1863)
British novellist and author.

NOVEMBER 7

The world is a looking-glass, and gives back to every man the reflection of his own face. Frown at it, and it in turn will look sourly upon you; laugh at it and with it, and it is a jolly, kind companion.

William Thackery

WILLIAM MAKEPEACE THACKERAY (1811-1863)
British novellist and author.

Wisdom for
Each Day

NOVEMBER 8

Am I mindful that the future will one day be the present?

Isaac L. Tigert

ISAAC LAGRONE TIGERT
(1892-1978)
Mississippi lawyer and politician.

NOVEMBER 9

Life is not so short but
that there is always time
enough for courtesy.

Ralph Waldo Emerson
<u>Social Aims</u>

RALPH WALDO EMERSON
(1803-1882)
American essayist, poet, and
lecturer.

Wisdom for
Each Day

NOVEMBER 10

That man is the richest whose pleasures are the cheapest.

Henry David Thoreau

HENRY DAVID THOREAU (1817-1862) American writer, abolitionist, and philosopher.

NOVEMBER 11

It is not enough to be industrious; so are the ants. What are you industrious about?

Henry David Thoreau

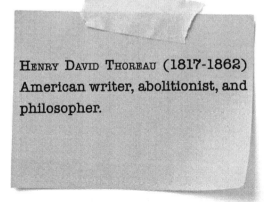

HENRY DAVID THOREAU (1817-1862) American writer, abolitionist, and philosopher.

November 12

The most I can do for my friend is simply be his friend. I have no wealth to bestow on him. If he knows that I am happy in loving him, he will want no other reward. Is not friendship divine in this?

Henry David Thoreau

HENRY DAVID THOREAU (1817-1862) American writer, abolitionist, and philosopher.

NOVEMBER 13

Make the most of your regrets. To regret deeply is to live afresh.

Henry David Thoreau

HENRY DAVID THOREAU (1817-1862) American writer, abolitionist, and philosopher.

NOVEMBER 14

There is so much good in the worst of us, and so much bad in the best of us, That it ill behooves any of us to find fault with the rest of us.

James Truslow Adams

JAMES TRUSLOW ADAMS (1878-1949)
American writer and historian.

November 15

It is sometimes expedient
to forget what you know.

Publilius Syrus

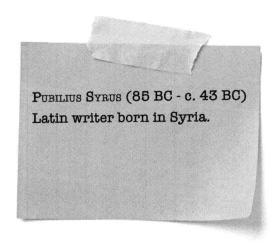

Publilius Syrus (85 BC - c. 43 BC)
Latin writer born in Syria.

Wisdom for
Each Day

NOVEMBER 16

Humor is the good-natured
side of truth.

Mark Twain

MARK TWAIN (1835-1910)
Pen name for Samuel Langhorne
Clemens: American humorist,
writer, and journalist.

NOVEMBER 17

Grief can take care of itself; but to get the full value of joy, you must have somebody to divide it with.

Mark Twain

MARK TWAIN (1835-1910)
Pen name for Samuel Langhorne Clemens: American humorist, writer, and journalist.

NOVEMBER 18

The human race has one
really effective weapon
and that is laughter.

Mark Twain

MARK TWAIN (1835-1910)
Pen name for Samuel Langhorne
Clemens: American humorist,
writer, and journalist.

NOVEMBER 19

One of the most important
trips a man can make is
that involved in meeting
the other fellow halfway.

Bruce Van Horn

This saying from Bruce Van Horn
was printed in the Daily Standard
newspaper in Sikeston, Missouri
on April 27, 1966.

Wisdom for
Each Day

November 20

Use what talents you possess; the woods would be very silent if no birds sang there except those that sang best.

Henry Van Dyke

HENRY VAN DYKE (1852-1933) American author and clergyman.

November 21

The best way to know God is
to love many things.

Vincent Van Gogh

VINCENT VAN GOGH (1852-1890)
Dutch painter.

November 22

For they can conquer who
believe they can.

Virgil

VIRGIL (70 BC - 19 BC)
Roman poet.

NOVEMBER 23

There can be no rainbow
without a cloud and a
storm.

John H. Vincent

JOHN H. VINCENT (1832-1920)
American bishop of the
Methodist Episcopal Church.

NOVEMBER 24

Our relationship to Christ
determines the kind of
light the world sees in us.

V.L. Vinhean

The identity of V.L. Vinhean
and the history of this epigram
is unknown.

NOVEMBER 25

Forsake not an old friend, for the new is not comparable unto him. A new friend is as new wine; when it is old though shalt drink it with pleasure.

Book of Sirach 9:10

BOOK OF SIRACH (ECCLESIASTICUS)
Apocryphal book included in the King James Bible until 1885 and is still included in the Catholic Bible.

Wisdom for
Each Day

NOVEMBER 26

The whole secret of life
is to be interested in one
thing profoundly and in
thousand other things well.

Hugh Walpole

HUGH WALPOLE (1884-1941)
British novelist, critic, and
dramatist.

NOVEMBER 27

Undertake not what you cannot perform but be careful to keep your promise.

George Washington

GEORGE WASHINGTON (1732-1799) Commander of the Continental Army and First President of the United States

Wisdom for
Each Day

NOVEMBER 28

Don't dwell on the negative,
excel in the positive.

Anonymous

The history of this anonymous
saying is unknown.

November 29

Don't tell me that worry doesn't do any good. I know better. The things I worry about don't happen.

The Watchman-Examiner

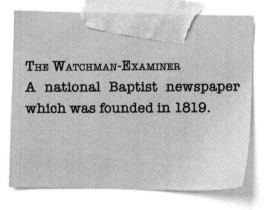

THE WATCHMAN-EXAMINER
A national Baptist newspaper which was founded in 1819.

NOVEMBER 30

Until a man has found God,
he begins at no beginning
and works to no end.

H.G. Wells

HERBERT GEORGE WELLS
(1866-1946)
British writer and historian.

DECEMBER

DECEMBER 1

Do all the good you can,
In all the ways you can,
In all the places you can,
At all the times you can,
To all the people you can,
As long as you ever can.

John Wesley

JOHN WESLEY (1703-1791)
British theologian responsible
for founding Methodism.

DECEMBER 2

There are two ways of
spreading light: To be the
candle, or the mirror that
reflects it.

Edith Warton

EDITH WHARTON (1862-1937)
American novelist and short
story writer.

DECEMBER 3

Never argue at the dinner table, for the one who is not hungry always gets the best of the argument.

Richard Whately

RICHARD WHATELY (1787-1863) British rhetorician, economist, theologian, and Archbishop of Dublin.

DECEMBER 4

Some folks just don't seem
to realize, when they're
moaning about not getting
prayers answered, that
"no" is the answer.

Nelia Gardner White

NELIA GARDNER WHITE (1894-1957)
American writer.

DECEMBER 5

The most difficult thing
in the world is to know
how to do a thing and to
watch somebody else doing
it wrong, without comment.

T. H. White

TERENCE HANBURY WHITE
(1906-1964)
British Arthurian author.

Wisdom for
Each Day

DECEMBER 6

Flowers are God's thoughts of beauty taking form to gladden mortal gaze. Lovely flowers are the smiles of God's goodness.

William Wilberforce

WILLIAM WILBERFORCE (1759-1833) British politician and leading abolitionist.

DECEMBER 7

Laugh and the world laughs
with you,
Weep and you weep alone,
For the sad old earth must
borrow its mirth,
But has trouble enough of
its own.

                    Ella Wheeler Wilcox

ELLA WHEELER WILCOX
(1850-1919)
American author and poet.

Wisdom for
Each Day

DECEMBER 8

Nothing endures but personal qualities.

Walt Whitman

WALT WHITMAN (1819-1892) American poet, journalist, and essayist.

DECEMBER 9

We search the world for truth; we cull
The good, the pure, the beautiful,
From all old flower fields of the soul;
And, weary seekers of the best,
We come back laden from our quest
To find that all the sages said
In the Book our Mothers read.

John Greenleaf Whittier

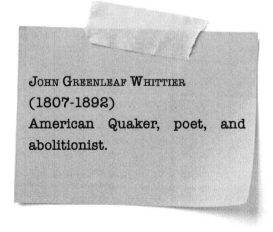

JOHN GREENLEAF WHITTIER
(1807-1892)
American Quaker, poet, and
abolitionist.

Wisdom for
Each Day

DECEMBER 10

God knows our strength; he
calls us to perform what
he knows we can do.

H.L. Wolfe

The identity of H.L. Wolfe and
the history of this epigram is
unknown.

December 11

Oh, to have the gift to think for ourselves as we can think for others!

Anonymous

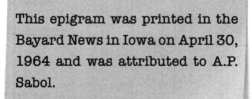

This epigram was printed in the Bayard News in Iowa on April 30, 1964 and was attributed to A.P. Sabol.

Wisdom for
Each Day

DECEMBER 12

Time is too slow for those who wait,
Too swift for those who fear,
Too long for those who grieve,
Too short for those who rejoice,
But for those who love, time is
eternity.

                        Henry Van Dyke

HENRY VAN DYKE (1852-1933)
American author and clergyman.

DECEMBER 13

You need glasses if you
never see some good
qualities in everyone.

Anonymous

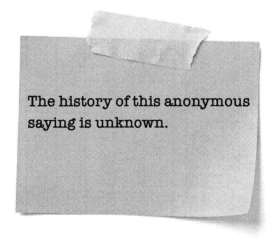

The history of this anonymous
saying is unknown.

DECEMBER 14

Don't let opportunity stare
you in the back instead of
in the face.

Anonymous

This anonymous saying was
printed in the Plano Daily Star-
Courier on September 6, 1956.

DECEMBER 15

If you are content with the best you have done, you will never do the best you can do.

Martin Vanbee

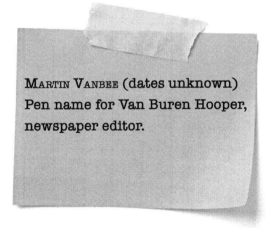

MARTIN VANBEE (dates unknown)
Pen name for Van Buren Hooper,
newspaper editor.

DECEMBER 16

If you see good in everybody,
nearly everybody will see
good in you.

Anonymous

This anonymous saying was
printed in the Coast Banker, a
newspaper devoted to Pacific
coast business interests, in
August 1922.

DECEMBER 17

Your friend is the man who knows all about you and still likes you.

Elbert Hubbard

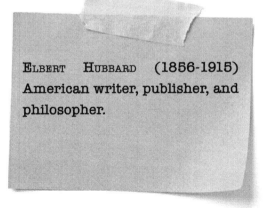

ELBERT HUBBARD (1856-1915) American writer, publisher, and philosopher.

DECEMBER 18

God grant me the serenity
To accept the things I
    cannot change;
The courage to change
    the things I can;
And the wisdom to know
    the difference.

Reinhold Niebuhr

KARL PAUL REINHOLD NIEBUHR
(1892-1971)
American theologian,
commentator, and professor.

DECEMBER 19

I find that the great thing
in this world is not so much
where we stand as in what
direction we are moving.

Oliver Wendell Holmes, Sr.

OLIVER WENDELL HOLMES, SR.
(1809-1894)
American physician, poet,
and father of U.S. Supreme
Court Justic Oliver Wendell
Holmes, Jr.

Wisdom for
Each Day

DECEMBER 20

All success is based on luck
but I've noticed the harder
I work the luckier I get.

Anonymous

This anonymous saying closely
resembles an epigram from
THOMAS JEFFERSON (1743-1826)
founding father and 3rd U.S.
President.

DECEMBER 21

Learning is like rowing
upstream; Not to advance
but to drop back.

Chinese Proverb

~

Words of wisdom from Chinese
antiquity.

~

Wisdom for
Each Day

DECEMBER 22

The most completely lost of
all days is that on which
one has not laughed.

Nicolas Chamfort

NICOLAR CHAMFORT (1741-1794)
French writer and secretary to
Louis XVI's sister.

DECEMBER 23

Happy the man and happy he alone,
He who can call today his own;
He who, secure within, can say
Tomorrow, do your worst;
I've lived today.

                    John Dryden

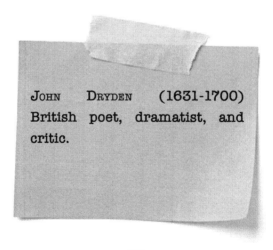

JOHN DRYDEN (1631-1700)
British poet, dramatist, and
critic.

Wisdom for
Each Day

DECEMBER 24

Help us O Lord! with patient
    love to bear
Each other's faults to suffer with
    true meekness
Help us each other's joys and
    griefs to share,
But let us turn to Thee alone
    in weakness.

Anonymous

This anonymous poem was published in the Friends' Intelligencer in Philadelphia on October 22, 1859.

DECEMBER 25

For unto you is born this day in the city of David, a Savior, which is Christ the Lord.

Luke 2:11

KING JAMES VERSION, HOLY BIBLE
The King James Bible was issued in 1611 by King James I and became the official Christian Bible for the Church of England.

Wisdom for
Each Day

DECEMBER 26

The world is like a mirror
Reflecting what you do
And if your face is smiling
It smiles right back at you.

Anonymous

This anonymous poem was
published in the Waunakee
Tribune Newspaper in Wisconsin
on September 15, 1966.

DECEMBER 27

We are not here to play,
    to dream and drift
We have work to do
    and loads to lift,
Shun not the struggle,
    face it, 'tis God's gift.

Maltbie Davenport Babcock

MALTBIE DAVENPORT BABCOCK
(1858-1901)
American theologian and
pastor.

DECEMBER 28

No man ever sank under the burden of the day. It is when tomorrow's burden is added to the burden of today that the weight is more than a man can bear.

George MacDonald

GEORGE MACDONALD (1824-1905) Scottish author, poet, Christian minister, and mentor to Lewis Carroll.

DECEMBER 29

Begin the day with God and
ask for his help.

Anonymous

The history of this anonymous
saying is unknown.

DECEMBER 30

Trust Him when dark doubts
assail thee,
Trust Him when trust is small,
Trust Him when simply to
trust Him
Is the hardest thing of all.

Dr. Wilfred Grenfell

DR. WILFRED GRENFELL (1865-1940)
British medical missionary.

DECEMBER 31

Forget the things that are behind;
Forget injuries, slight, unkind words,
Be too big to be hurt,
Be too great to be unkind;
Be too busy to quarrel,
Too wise to engage in unseemly gossip,
Too strong to permit little annoyances to
turn you from life's big road;
Too clean to stain your character with
any kind of impurity.

Anonymous

This saying was printed in the
Vidette-Messenger of Porter
County in Indiana on June 3,
1939.

My great-grandfather, Richard Hayes Burgess
June 3, 1885 - March 18, 1976

82644820R00248

Made in the USA
Middletown, DE
04 August 2018